When A Cafe Door Opens

VOLUME 2
JULY-DECEMBER

© 2020, Elizabeth Martina Bishop
No part of this book november be reproduced without permission.
Requests for permission to reproduce selections of this book should be mailed to:

Elizabeth Martina Bishop, Ph.D.
2675 West State Route 89A, #1100
Sedona, AZ 86336, USA

ISBN: 9798561976759

BISAC: Nonfiction / Poetry / Women Authors

www.ElizabethMartinaBishop.com

Design by Artline Graphics, Sedona AZ, USA
www.artline-graphics.com

When A Cafe Door Opens

VOLUME 2

JULY-DECEMBER

ELIZABETH MARTINA BISHOP

TABLE OF CONTENTS

JULY

AUGUST

SEPTEMBER

OCTOBER

NOVEMBER

DECEMBER

POEM FOR ALL SEASONS

Gratitude
Reckoning up
Seasonal accounts
In winter,
Defined by mountain
Fathered by thistledown feather
Snow-trodden weather
Yet no tracks are windswept
Brokered by snow bunting bird

In spring,
Bathe in crescendo
Of light soothing and consoling
In raw blossoming
Of flower petals
Burnished truth
Incarnadine
Held to ransom
In a far-off bower's fairy ring
Or by tongue of scythe
Flung wide of the mark

In autumn harvest
Garbed in surround
Of leaf-mound,
Countless lives
Totted up

How many
Russet wings
In inked in ledger-books
Of pages, ambushed, published,
Turning into alchemical gold

In summer, leaning, widowed,
Stooped shoulder of countless goddess
Hastening past waterfalls of rushing water
Countless the number of lightning strikes
Flying under patrol of sky-parasol

July

Inside Every Old Person There's A
Young One Struggling to Get Out

JULY 1

It seemed to me when you began
Reading these poems
You were well on your way
To going to sleep.
Your eyes
Began to tremble
As a preamble
To a different sort
Of astral travel.
Trembling in their sockets,
Although heavy-lidded,
Lids were closing,
And everything might have been
Natural, still I wanted to make sure
You'd come back.
In fact, your eyes had the look
Of one who was already asleep,
Or eyes that would radiate
That faraway look
That says I have been
Visiting other kingdoms
Edged with tombs
Jewels are that are now
Or have been
Obsolete, are housed
In a new museum featuring
Treasures gathered from

Wherever the whereabouts
Of Agamemnon's
Or Tutankhamen's tombs.

When I looked out on the patio,
I looked askance at everything.
There is an absence
That is overwhelming
Now that the animals have left.
I am sure a local circus owner
Did the downright dirty on us
Because no wild animal
Would ever look at us
As of we were part of an entourage
Of items from the local zoo,
Like as wherever they were from.
I don't even know
Where that was
All I know is that
And mother lynxes
Never growl and allow
Their kittens
To climb pine trees
As they were playing
In Kensington Gardens
On jungle gyms
Put up by the local charity
And it was not during a season
Of Covid or the Spanish Flu
Or anything resembling
A pandemic lockdown.

Besides, when I saw the gypsy
Explaining to a cameraman
As to how to make French toast
With a Bunsen burner for an oven
And by cracking the shells
Of a couple of quail eggs
It was a way of saying
The bride price had spiraled down
To an incredible lockdown price
Beyond any previously known
Showdown known in history
To subsets of dowry-makers
So low at the time of this writing,
The council was going
To look into whether
They could outlaw
Or go forward to disallow
Dowries offered on the account
Of the Bulgarian bride market
Becoming gang-infested
With motorcycles and such
And people sabotaging tradition
By booking dates on line
And buying dresses
That didn't extend
Down to the ground
As was required

By those familiar
With the tenets of tradition.
Besides the eldest boy
Kept saying
I'm not doing it
While he was ogling
At his cell phone
But he was having dates
With women
And this is not where
The story ends right there at all.
Those internet girls
Coming apart at the seams
Did not even know
He was a renegade
From the Bulgarian bridal market
That he was still in the habit
Of luring
Some unsuspecting brides
Who were common settled folks?
Not Romany lavengro lil
Tell me if some of them
Would have some of it when none
Of them would opt to have any of it anyway?
And who had absolutely no inkling?
As to what was to follow
Since the handsomest bloke in the world

As well as his working parents
Were one hundred percent gypsy.

Don't ever ask why we are gone?
Where we are going?
You said we would head
Sunward for that hill
I do not think we will.
Rain falls on the graves
Of the departed.
He always takes us for Rumanians.
We used to wait for the train
For over ten hours
Just to get home.
Why was my other manuscript?
Messed up. Don't even ask
A bloke was heard to say
A lot is riding on this *crème de menthe*.
I have often wanted an orchid
To grow at home.
We have already done
Whatever it is we wanted.
We are treading water
At this time.
The dog-paddle
Would be good enough.
I hear my daughter
Once again teasing me
And bullying:

Mom, are you scared

Of skinny dipping.
From the moment of her birth
She always had the upper hand.
But over what? Her mother?
Has she no respect for herself?
You always
Have that impulse
To close the book
Of the dancer.
Under what circumstances
Do you write those poems?
What do you do
To prepare for the writing
Of them proper.
There is great loss
Everywhere.
People are spitting out
Watermelon seeds
Everywhere.

The interview went
Very badly at first.
I was coughing the entire time.
The interviewer never relented
In her attack mode.
Hellbent she was
On where she was taking me
Down the road and a few other places
Where no one could ever have caught
Sight of what she was doing or even why.
There are moments when words
Fail me and the body breaks
Into pieces of bread
And you no longer
Believe in the story of loaves and fishes.
The woman also refused
To even bring me a glass of water.
She preferred to leave me coughing.
Then the same woman asked me:
What happened
To your husband?
Wasn't he some type
Of a lawyer?
So, couldn't he have put a stop
To all this caterwauling if he had wanted?
I said: didn't he try to strangle me
Of a Sunday morning?

Why should I live in a hovel?
Didn't this occur at the time
There wasn't even
Any war going on
In Afghanistan?
Somehow doesn't that fact make
All of it, all right,
Or does it?

July 6

The waitress says
Fully expecting
One day to become
An airplane pilot,
She has that easy devil-well-may-care
Attitude that makes flying
Her palace of grace, her coven of air.
The freedom of outer and inner space.
Is that how it is explained
By those in the know?
If her boyfriend admits to the truth:
That cannot add or subtract.
He will beat up anyone
Whoever dares cross-examine her motives
In the restaurant business.
If someone happens to make a comment:
She has fine legs or a great smile.
That individual will soon realize
The sacrifice accorded those
Considered a part
Of the ritual of baptism,
The occasion of senseless funerals.
And the communion of saints.
He says, if she happens
To make a mistake
Regarding a bit of computation
Concerning an extra difficult part of a bill,

So be it. She's not perfect,
But she's the perfect partner in bed,
How that activity openly turns out.
Is what is expected
Of all women everywhere.
That's the reason
Women have been placed on earth,
Not in a heavenly corral
Since there are other commonalities
Concerning additional errors
Or, other kinds of mistakes
Of which people have sometimes have
Shown they are capable,
While living in drought conditions,
When passing the marmalade,
Across the breakfast table,
One might be called upon
Or be somewhat inclined to ask:
What is it about the flirtation?
With Boeing?

JULY 7

The theme of the survival trial
Would you do it again?
If a dog is offered a bone
And accepts it
Will he do anything
Just to get Kristy that reward?
Or, will he do only so much,
Or as little as possible
And still grab the bone,
Pain is a bit like that,
Excruciating before the reward
Of no pain.
The point
To bob-sledding,
To hit the snow
And take whatever comes.
Looking at the dog,
In performance mode
No one knows
By chance
If the dog
Named Wendy
Remotely
Controlled?
After all, it appears
Willingly he speaks
In five languages.

As it is, ventriloqual
Acts are mostly the same,
The same operettas
Played over and over again.
What about the law of averages?
When they are played over and over
During the course of our lives,
Don't our lives resemble
The lost lives of Paul of Tarsus?
The number of times we intone:
We do not presume
To come to this thy table, Lord,
The number of times
We wash the kitchen floor
At home.
What are the keys
Causing us to resist
Arrest?
Our fatal flaws
Binding us to the lost laws
Of temptation?
Adhering to the rose
Or the thorn trees
In the park,
In old age,
Life ends up
Being the same
Under lockdown.

July 8

My great aunt asks:
What is your
Philosophy of life?
I ask: why do you
Want to know?
I'm only five years old.
I am not aware
She is a theosophist
And a twin.
That makes a difference
To how she thinks
About the blowing of the wind,
The parasol of pine trees
That, without exception,
Will later lift me
Straight off the ground
By how many feet
I have no idea,
Not within the confines
Of this traditional surround.
When she hands
Me embroidered
Dinner napkins
With orange hydrangeas on them,
My mother removes them
From my person.

All activities
Of giving or receiving
Are like that
In a childhood
Of remorse
And deprivation.
I don't know why.
It is often like that,
Objects seem to move
Around a lot,
Not so much
Around surfaces
On the dinner table
But on the table
With rickety legs
Placed in the hall
So, everyone can see
The carefully embroidered
Dinner mats a sign of immortal
Handiwork and bliss,
Meant as a peace offering
In a family whose heirlooms
Never caught sight of again.
Do hiccoughs
Personify
The inner debate
Surrounding bliss?
Is there something else?
What of the interior life,
Stoked by inertia's fitful flames,
The quarrelsome universe
Disbelieving of itself.
The entire day, shot to hell.

Everyone else's edition
Of suffering morose,
Full of remorse,
As well as everything else.
Banish the self
From the borderlands
Of infinity
Lest one become drunk
On the wine of infinity.

JULY 9

Karma cancels out
The wine-press of the self,
The sky cries for help.
Stars appear to weep.
In an of themselves
Planets protest.
The burning sun
Planetary influences
Guide us
With the sweet perfume
Of a manuscript
Enlisting the senses
Providing us
With their own
Horoscope,
Blasting each
Of the tavern windows,
Where blossoms
Once bloomed
Without hesitation,
Why did they continue
When they were there
Just for the asking
Of nothingness,
Emptiness, despair,
An Angelic Being
Always singing.

Is she too,
Of the nothingness
Of air?
So does the guest
Enter the garden
Scattering stars
Everywhere.
Is hidden light
Ruthless
As divine reproof?

JULY 10

The charnel ground
Swept clean of spring snow
Thawing
The desert
Swept clean
Of lizard
Quicksilver
Upon an adobe wall
The raven
Who cawed
And sang his way
Past the beginning of time
Where everything
Begetting a terrifying crossroads,
The time when
Everything hellbent on descension's crown.
If we saw through the veils
Why then is the interfering
Canticle of aloofness
Always misunderstood?
Waves tilt,
The fire of wisdom melts.

JULY 11

When our hotel room burned down
In Galway, we got a trailer.
The resulting headlines
In the local newspaper read:
        HIPPY COUPLE
        MEET IN HIP HOP TRAILER.
We didn't even know our trailer
Was one of those aforesaid mentioned dives.
The bride was a Dublin Drama student,
He was the head of Pace College In New York.
They were in love and it was the Hippy Shop
In Galway did it.
He dived into a swimming pool.
After that he was from a group home in New Jersey.
I saw the bride once and she was just the same
But he was in a special home for paraplegics.
Why did a perfectly good marriage
Go bust? You cannot even imagine such a tragedy!
Meanwhile, yesterday the little old lady from Des Moines, Iowa,
With curls held in tight blonde fists to her head yesterday
She wore a celebrated British gingham print,
One that Aunt Kate would wear.
I'm sure this little old lady, though,
She would never ever
Be caught dead
Talking to the likes of us.
I'm going to Galway, Ireland she announced.

Without a bridge game, I knew I had been trounced.

I'm not going to die anytime soon.

I'll know when the time comes that I've had enough.

I used to work in the ICU Department of Insanity.

Until I reach the ripe old age of one hundred and twenty-five,

You won't see me going anytime soon.

True to whippersnapper internet form,

People simply do not talk like that today,

Or, off-set, are they sometimes caught unaware?

Acting less than cognizant of the vegetative state

Many people have been left to die in, to date?

It may be a very sorry insult to those who've gone before,

Especially war veterans and their relatives

Who must mourn the cost of war the rest of their lives?

Who would want to live that long? I questioned her

And held my head to one side like a bird.

I am one of a series of disciples of Doctor Hawkins she said.

To me that was like saying she was The Lone Ranger's sidekick.

Wouldn't you just know it! I would say instead

Of using an well-known Irish expression, fancy!

Or instead, fancy that! Or, can you just imagine?

Meanwhile, as my most well-endowed and vibrant spirit guide,

My mother used to say:

Wisdom comes from around small places

From small people in generous doses.

Bully, bully for you!

Bully, bully for me!

If you're as old as I am,

You may have heard that song.

Having met the little old lady courtesy of a dark alley,

I stepped aside for her, timidly and knowingly.

Because of meeting such a powerful medium,

To show her a decent modicum of respect,

I wanted to let her go out of the door first.
Upon seeing our inborn version of humility,
She copped an attitude: What is wrong? She confessed.
Would she understand the makings of this poem?

JULY 12

Today, I saw the elf who had a small a Xmas elf
Pinned to her lapel by me over six years ago.
She is from New Hampshire. Out here, in cowpoke country
The Eastern accent stands out. The elf often works
At the Thrifty Nickel. Her entire life is metaphorical.
Even without a mask, I did not recognize her, oh so sad!
She is a woman who does only good works.
She is on the shop floor to serve only the poor.
When she saw me leaning out of the window
Of that great big blue truck,
She looked at me with such a wry smile, I knew I had hurt her.
I knew something was really wrong and that riding around
In the truck was giving her knees a true case of lumbago.
Most people forget elves and do not even know
Why elves incarnate.
I know she must have thought—
Even though, it's not even Christmas,
Elizabeth does not recognize elves.
Pretty sad stuff to contemplate!
Now the elf might be thinking to herself:
Though, at one time in the past,
Elizabeth pinned a little charm and replica
Of an elf (myself) on my lapel
At one time, though she honored me,
Perhaps she now feels guilty.

JULY 13

The door of the tavern is open but I am up and down
And is and is not inhabits my psyche. I have emptied out
All of my closets, I have sold all my suitcases.
As soon as I did that,
I wanted to escape.
To live somewhere else would be a boon.
Blasphemy slips through the open door.
Hinges allow the wrong kind of door to swing either way.
Felled the fruit tree whispers
Of mortality's weary strategy.
Is there anywhere I can hide?
Soul windows have cracked with cosmic light.
Is the innkeeper's bride
An angel? The shallow cup is overturned.
I yearn for eternity's teacup.

July 14

One companion dreams of my defeat.
Another person dreams of my reward.
How many people are walking in and out of
From the walls of the art gallery?
Soul-tossed, soul-drenched with light,
How will rings of evanescent light dim?
How much must I live and dwell in blindness to be forgiven?
Predestined
Is the dust of contemplation's vast desert
Winking from the golden lake of sun.

JULY 15

He went back every day after his beloved died.
He demanded the medium bring back his beloved
In a frightening lightening flash that was binding to the flesh.
He was a most demanding client that had ever lived,
That was because he loved his beloved more than average.
She did the best that she could,
Money could not assuage the allure
Of sinecure and the cure for his lovesick madness.
Lonely, he was overwrought with sadness.
The warp and weft, the weave of love could not
Be rewoven overnight. He thought it could.
He saw a rainbow in the sky. This was a sign.
He then saw another woman,
Slender and bright she was.
He slicked down his hair.
That suddenly and abruptly ended
All his trips to the spirit medium.
Now he entered another dimension.
Saplings daubed with a hint of jasmine perfume
Spoke to him of the beauty of his second beloved.
In truth, he thought his new beloved
The same as his former beloved lass.
Though he saw through the transparent
Gaze of the master, and though he knew
He himself was not the master
He thought he could command
To the portals of heaven to open.

Love has drowned him in a fragile cup.
On the brim of as shallow wine-cup
He pressed his lips and related what he did:
I cannot live like this. I want to die.
He read the sum total of all the old books
From the past and wept brave tears.
How eloquent had been the wedding in the garden!
Until all of the pages, extinguished and burned
In one divine reading, he learned he was finished
His life on earth had no meaning. And, as a nightingale
Sung of one hundred torches and one hundred stories
Every song was sung from the heart of greater good.
No one knew exactly what that was,
One of life's greatest mysteries, alas!

JULY 16

What has been dreamt into shape
Cannot be written and rewritten.
The sadness of broken dreams
Rendered the man almost inhuman
Silent as a sultan on a throne.

The omniscience of the lamp of human kindness
Blinds me. I have closed the door of the innkeeper's house,
To what avail? Release documents demanded from everyone.
Copious attention placed on every dotted syllable proclaimed.
I never said what I said. I never did what I did.
I only swam the river of blindness once.
My soul was only printed in a second-hand edition,
The last edition
I never edited so it belonged to someone else, purloined
And marketed in dinars. The rate of exchange fluctuates.
I stamp on the grapes and still there is no alchemical condition
Which reveals the distance between two grape vineyards:
The law of cause and effect is hidden.

July 18

Lockdown is followed by lockdown.
Close down the innkeeper's tavern
And everyone drowns in monotony's crown.

JULY 19

First you offered me a car.

Then you offered me your sofa.

Then you ordered me to write

Or pen a sample verse.

Money never came into it.

Here, sit down you cried, come sit down on my red leather sofa

Take up this pen and lend me a sample of *Feathers in the Wind.*

Your wise-woman's wisdom's tears may dissuade

Or allay all my fears of loneliness.

So, I penned these lines:

> *I have approached the black-legged egret with regret.*
> *My sense of loss is never-ending.*
> *I keen the crooning voices in the marshland.*
> *The cicadas will not end my sense of lament,*
> *Never-ending, once again. Amen.*

Ah ha! you cried, your verse is not one iota,

Not one jot like hers, it is one hundred percent

Dissimilar to my beloved's outpouring of love and devotion

For divinity's spiritual fable and limitless flame.

Your verse fails weigh in as worth an ounce of silver or gold.

If even what the dead have died

For what now prospers in a new dimension,

Love lies undefended from cudgels

Fashioned from blameless remorse, and regret,

Or a sense of love, grief-stricken.

If lanterns flicker in an unmet wind of longing,

What is it will congeal or heal

The sutured threads of consciousness?
No vaudeville stand-in can add or subtract stories even
Comparable to parables of the flesh.
In a season of summer, even the most unfavorable gazelle
Of my beloved's stanza and sutras
Can easily clear the roof from the template
Of your temple or palace.
Thus, though your attempt at verse, brazen at best,
Will always fail
Mesh with the travail of crepuscular inconsistencies,
Fickle, foolhardy, due to your spells of choleric disposition,
Your lack of loyalty
Indicative of an unseemly state of grammar
In this terrain and country's surround,
For me to forgive or even mutter forgiving words such as,
Live and let live,
That would be taken as an oversight, and, as such,
A travesty of justice!
Moving past such an exclusionary
And meandering sense of prejudice,
A Persephone trespassing and
Traversing the depths of my keening soul,
Your pen is blackened with a history of regret,
Malfeasance, indicative of self-pity at its worst.
Considering the bell-tolled pilgrimage
To and from the spiritual household.
Since Rumi's last wedding night,

You have fallen into disfavor and dishonor.
What's even worse, you will not admit
To the allowance of god's spiritual divinity.
How can you put out: words to the effect,
Within and without, you're not even an imposter
Of a very fine lady. Of a very high station she was.
In consideration of her royal status,
Your verses have been better days.
Instead, they reflect absolutely nothing
But an aperture to melancholic and morose melodies,
Indignities avoiding
Embarrassment or embellishment in embroideries
Exhibiting further mayhem.
Disallowing for seeds of further mayhem,
Why not admit the truth?
You have nothing of note to offer a sultan of poetry.
Not even to a suzerain
Of a fief or to kingdom or even to a man held in high regard,
A doctor, to boot.
Instead, the meagre offering imputed to your signature,
Append as samples of pale
Mosaic tableaux stolen from Psyche's
Vast subterranean underworld.
Further, as for the jewels you wea,
Those appear to belong to an idolator's coroner.
I answered: my verse was never put forward
Or stated anything like hers.
I have no master. All the days of my life,
No humbling of reality prospers here
Pass by me like idling rivulets of fire.
My days, my hours fleeting in the grip
Of idolatrous schemes.
Impertinence is my master and my sister to grief's mirror.

As for the cup of wine,

I have never known the source of impermanence.

A creeping sense of extinction inhabits most of my prayers

Whispered beneath quilts.

The source, the origin of what I'm writing is lost.

Too delicate a flower

I am to view the blooming of the rose on the hillside.

Self-indulgent, before seeking your holy presence.

I've lain down winding sheets

Across all of my prized possessions of furniture.

I am not garbed in mourning garments

Like the rest, but I am still mourning the life of

The same woman whom you mourn.

I am keening the same wounds

That you have accrued from knowing her.

What you have known of her holy presence, I have known.

My mission the same as yours.

I can only weep I am not even she nor even a divine rishi

Or one who is paid to keen.

I don't even wait tables.

Nor do I carry a tray nor balance a vase over my head.

My bewilderment ebbs and flows in the way

Of tidal waters subsumed,

Granted, taken on by the moon swimming in its own reflection,

Heart-felt and muted.

The dark wires, the vines of my conscience,

My sense of inner loyalty

Will never allow me to consider conjoining my soul to yours.

The gate-keeper is done with his penultimate charade.

I have no teeth. My boat is overturned.

All the rivers of blood have turned to stone.

July 20

Today, the only thing that defines us is the weather.
When we correct poems, she has this clipboard.
That's the table of contents. I have the poems.
She has the annotated comments. I only have
One other book entitled Codfish on a Tin Plate
So, I thought it fitting to educate the reader
About the need to know what the poem is about
That is why I thought to pen Enough Bird Song to Go Around
When these days, there isn't enough song to go around anywhere.
Because what is happening around in the state of New Mexico
Songbirds are dropping like flies.
Not only that over three hundred species
Of birds have recently disappeared.
We are not talking whales here
Or passenger pigeons.
Some people prefer short stories
To poetry so I wanted to make sure
I could expand the readership.
Once a person accused me of calling a poem
A short story when a poem is not a short story.
Oh well, I said. You can call a poem derivative
 Of something else. Specifically, in short, and
For example, you can call a poem a sampling
Of narrative verse. Each poem, then, if we hope,
It's any good at all, after all, should tell a story.

How to correct a poem is quite simple.
Is to place Cleo on the red, leather sofa
With a clipboard and let it fly out
Of her large hands, at least, once
Every ten minutes, one poem at a time
Or thereabouts. Synchronicity.
The next thing is to establish
Abbreviated titles for the table of contents
And actual titles for the poems and matching
Actual titles for the abbreviated titles
As well as for the annotations.
The next thing is to make sure the annotations are
Full of hot gossip or something you
Could never deduce only from a flat reading
A poem. In this way, the reader will come
To believe the poem is an accurate example
Of the habit of social distancing and masking
Occurring between the words of each poem. Also, the annotations
Should reflect the inadequate scholarship
Of the poet and make sure followers
In the readership know that, although a former academic,
The poet is no longer an academic, especially
When it comes to poetry, but more of a free-flowing
Type of an artist who is prepared to sacrifice
Issues of longevity for the impromptu
And spontaneous performance of aesthetics
Of art, music, and dance, probably in that order.

JULY 22

Making poetry corrections and edits.
Is a horrendous hair-pulling experience.
So, first Cleo reads the poem aloud
On a tape-recorder. Then Elizabeth
Follows with an off-set off-color reading
Of the poem. One notes where the words
Are difficult to spit out due to Covid
Restrictions. We wear masks during
This process because though some words
Are over-selected with great care from
The store-house of creativity, in reality
Really a convenience store down the road,
Are extremely difficult to pronounce.
Especially without teeth and due
To the highest number, hand-picked,
Comprised of alliterative poetic fallacies.

July 23

When I took my ex-husband
To the Spiritualist Church
In November, straightaway, he fainted dead away.
Right in the front aisle of the church corridor,
He passed out to his great blush and embarrassment.
That did it, insofar as religion and politics
Were concerned him.
When he came to, he stated
Due to overwork and burn-out, all his karma
Had magically been sheared away
From the platelets of his body.
In another life, he believed
Deeply in spiritualist principles
But not during one day in this life.
Inclusive of all his eccentricities
And belief systems, from now on,
He said he would live the life
Of a country gentleman
And visit art galleries,
Indulge in fine dining,
And attend poetry readings.
A darling afficionado of the art world
Because of his recurring patronage,
He said he owed me nothing.
That I was no longer an interest
Of his even though I walked
Ten miles over a thin sheet of ice

Barefoot just to get him to make a come back

And return to Ireland and get him out of England.
Even though he pulled The Last Judgement card,
He never seemed comfortable with his hedonist
Belief system and the Golden Rule. It was more like
If you mess up and use the wrong word,
It's up to you to imitate someone who once cared.
But now he doesn't have to. Money never ever
Seemed to come into the equation. Marry me
Or else was not the loving option of his deception.

July 24

I don't believe in the abyss.
But many people do and need to identify
With the terror of the night sky
And what is going in the world
That is part of a blind massive movement
Of many groups of unsavory people
Who are very far from enlightened,
Even though they go through
The merry-go-round motions
And extracurricular notions
Of eschewing politics, the church;
Then, too, there is always the judiciary.
Such folks want a selection of poems
Written out that are of the Hallowed-Be-Thy-Name
Variety of terror. Without let up, I write poems
Because I want to be an example to the rain-maker community.
The shopkeeper said it. I didn't.
Truly, I figure if I keep on fiercely
Writing poems, eventually it will rain cats and dogs.
In that case, the entire country scorched by fire
Might become lousy with torrents of rain.
In that case, all the precincts of the country will become
Saturated with lily-of-the-valley, forsythia,
Other priceless posies
Bursting forth from disused and now freshened clods of earth.
Yesterday, there were three incidents and events
Worthy of a diatribe descriptive of a few sprinkles

Afterwards, after things getting somewhat fired up.
Well, then, prune-like, the grey sky just dried up again.
The praying mantis acted like an eagle.
The rodent acted like a field mouse
And then the fire ants acted as if they heard my call
And came running into the living room poetry salon
To burn all of my toes, one by one.
It seemed very much
As if they were carrying miniature red-hot tongs
And flags stating: this is not the end of the pandemic
And this was not at all due to it being suddenly suggested
I had ever been a dyslexic or had dipped into the pages
Of a book entitled *The Plague* by someone called Camus.

JULY 25

Just as long as you know
You decided to opt for this perfect experience
And it really was truly an experiment
And if the doctors ever say
She has to do anything extra like pay
Or go through this experience again
She will definitely say no this time
Not like what happened last time
And not like now when she lost all her hair
And she had to be concurrent with that idea
And get a haircut when nit was the right time,
Whatever we forget in the wake of memory's face
Is the very thing that has saves us in the end
It definitely does not matter what time of day it was
Or exactly what day of the week
Thanks be to god again and again and then again
She says she thinks
She has a welcoming committee
Waiting for her up there in heaven
When the time comes and that is not now
But later whenever that is and it
Doesn't really matter when that is
Any more if not now, then, when, later
Is fully enough to contend with the spirits
And she said she also saw some kind of angel
And some kind of a man who was tall very tall
Whose name was Robert.

She is sure all the torch-bearing
Cicadas were behind her and urging her on
From now on, her life will be lived differently
She is sure she will be grateful
Herself has come back to herself
And every granule of sand
Makes sense to her now
Especially for the fact for her
Having been healed in the way she was
At such a dangerous juncture
Due to the miraculous appearance
In the shower and it was all over in there
A few times but she is still sure I myself
Still don't know anything about spoon-bending
Cleo says this is fine as it exists for the benefit
Of my bright sheltering undercover
But everyone is sheltering from some storm
Or other just now so it is ridiculous
To make assumptions. You just have to fend
 For yourself about anything going on that is important
She says also she is sure she didn't see
Anything when she reached nirvana
But she usually just senses things and doesn't see
What about the land of the tunnel and the palace of air?
Well, she says she is not afraid of death anymore.
She is also surprised that she is successful
In achieving a sense of identity standing in the water
Right up to the height of her waist.
And she says she is totally understanding of the fact the undertow
Will not necessarily pull you out to the center of the mesa of water
Or to the sea anymore unless you and she really want to go there

They have not announced their wedding
She plays the violin at other people's weddings
And that is all there is to it.
They say they will go to France
Later on, but he has not popped the question.
At my expense, the conversation will continue.

Madame Green Sea Turtle
Is crawling along the sea coast bedding down
To lay her eggs. Her shell
Is crepuscular like the dawn
Striped with painted lines of light.
Setting her sights on love,
She finds her mouth is full of seaweed.
At whatever time she lets herself down,
 She flops down on the sand,
She is whatever remains
Of her Beloved Ocean.
You've never understood
What those barriers are.

JULY 28

The windows are covered
With morning glories
And flower boxes
Full of creeping vines
The moon has this drunkard's habit
Of hovering for a while and then hanging out over the land.
This poem has been coming closer and closer
For many years.
Something fierce has been taking over:
This lover's madness.
The world is now set free
To break up into little islands of seaweed.
Why be known of such grief?

July 29

God says you do not deserve
This house, nor this quiet interlude.
At four o'clock in the morning
A child and her mother
Decide to take a stroll
In the exactitude of space where the mountain lions
Were sworn off the patio and back into the arroyo.
What were these two thinking?
Quiet, the old ladies are dreaming,
The mother comforts the strident
Tone of her child.
Human beings no longer lament their choices
They have made. All we see is a late moon's palest eye.
There may be a better place for us to have gone.
For a while it looked like we might get away.
Next time, let's make a better call
About what it was we wanted
And then stay.

JULY 30

This year I want to opt out
Of a birthday celebration.
I'd' rather watch the children
Kicking a ball around
In an open field we've filled with dreams of youth.
Even if the hermit is not here
It does not mean he is burned alive at the stake.

July 31

A man shot a moose in the heart.
He didn't kill him exactly, though.
Two hours later, the moose returns
And gores the man. No one says a thing.
Both of them are now deceased.
Sometimes a twin stays with us
For a little while
Notices the significance of the other
And then departs in silence.
Don't you think the moose
Was bellowing and asking for forgiveness.
The man never asked to take his life.
Today, both have found
Their way trembling
Towards an unknown heaven.
The cobblestones up there,
Hoof marks, everything,
Even the streets were paved in gold.

August

The Older the Fiddle,
the Sweeter the Tune

AUGUST 1

One summer before I left
We moved to Ipswich.
We went to Crane's Beach.
That summer I danced
The part of Giselle.
One of the Preston Boys
Came to watch.
I was crying
As I danced
The Mad Scene.
My mother took
The boy away
Out of the room
Where he was watching.
She told him:
My daughter's
Always been like that.
Something out of this world.

When I moved away,
My mother had it all planned.
I was to look
After Preston's sister, Julie
Who later emerged
As a very smart and hip
Commentator for NPR.
Now Preston's sister,

Julie, used to cry
About a lot of things
Not right with her life.
When I tried to make
Julie finish
Her homework
On John Smith
And Pocahontas.
Off stage, out in the hinterlands
Of the family living room,
Looking over
The nastiness
Of the spat,
A mother cat
Stood trembling
Waiting to pounce,
And, well, she did.
Had I not taken
Julie's kitten
Away for day
Because,
At ten years old,
Julie was expected
To finish
Her homework.
Though the rules had been
Made known to me
The day I had been hired.
At thirteen, I judged Julie
By my own standards,
The next thing
That happened,
I was fired.

Had nothing happened,
I'd probably have a job today.
I often wondered why
Verta Mae Grosvenor
Became a friend of mine
But the day she was to interview
My daughter for the class of _____,
My mother cancelled the interview.
Julia's mother, Julianna
An Atlantic Monthly
Superstar, was quick
To throw me out
Of the family home,
A brownstone.
So, that was how
I ended up
At Wyattville,
A boarding house.
My step mother always
Kept an arsenal of friends
Around like that,
When she was in a jam,
They came in handy.
In that way, everything
Was fake news.

One time
Something went wrong
With the Houdini act
A man was put
In a coffin length box
Handcuffed, strapped in
And hoisted to a third story
Level by two men climbing ladders
But when the coffin
Was coming down
And the man was expected
To reach ground level
It got stuck
How could the man
End up in the judges' corner?
An actor,
Wasn't he reenacting
The actual details of Houdini's death
That occurred underwater
When he could not escape
His watery tomb?
That's what took away Houdini's
Charmed life and star power.
At least he was able
To later communicate
From his grave
With his wife

Who always stood by him
And his
His assertions
He was a miracle man
Though now he'd ended up
Only as a disincarnate voice
Inebriated with offshore drowning
In salt water.

Later,
Claiming his son
Was the reincarnation
Of the actual star Houdini
A father
Brought his son
To a hotel
The son looked.
Rather ordinary to me.
By looking at him,
You just could not tell
Very much at all
Or anything extraordinary
Or miraculous about him.
Had he been a healer
Or a gospel singer,
I would have been
More interested.
Seemed like the father
Was a huckster of some sort
I recall one of the things
The father said about his son.
Non-plussed, some of
The audience members
Appeared completely taken in.
To back up his presentation,

About his wunderkind,
The father said
He found out
His son
Was very easily able to decode
The great giant statues
Strategically
Placed on Easter Island.

I don't know
Why it is against the law
To fall down
In the street.
I think one day
I was probably
Struck by lightning.
Anyway, when the police
Brought me to a hospital
For observation
And put me in restraints
And handcuffs
What happened later,
What I was able to do
Did this prove
Was I also Houdini?.
On account of my doing
Something
A little different
Then I'd been previously
Been accustomed to do:
I began performing what may
Be considered as any number of things
Pertaining to a welcoming dance,
One of those dances
Of a hula hoop variety
That children learn

When they are very young and holy.
I now recognize what I was doing
Was probably part
Of a Comanche dance
Practiced for centuries.
Thus, by moving securely
Inside the restraints
And imagining
An outsider's inside requirements
Or the reverse of that, of a dance
Leading to a hoop dancer's
Making an entrance at a parish hall.
I was able to completely free myself
Of the restraints. Now I was barefoot
And running past a sleeping hospital attendant
And giving a fast running chase
For twenty blocks
On hard cement pavement
Afterwards,
All things be equal,
In the eyes of god,
When I fell backwards
From the sky
And into the waiting arms
Of a policeman,
I wondered why
Why god in his great glory

Would be the only Master
Out of heaven
Allowing me to be caught.
On his part, allowing this to happen
Was the very thing
Changing
The entire course
Of my life story
Now I was emerging from
A semi restricted detour
And deprivation
Of a hospital
Waiting room
Into
A manacled
And shackled
Mode of operation?

AUGUST 5

When Marion and Bob
Came to visit
I asked them to tell
The waiter
Why I didn't come to work
At *The Crooked Mushroom Café and Restaurant*
Where I worked
Until last Saturday
When I was prevented
From coming to work
Because I fell in the street
Bob and Marion
Looked the same.
Auntie Mame
Was still Auntie Mame
But I was different.
They had given
Me medication
That eventually
Would kill me
In my sleep.
The rashes
Hadn't come up yet.
Since Bob was the cause
Of my running away
And Marion was the cause
Of my wanting to marry him

In the first place,
They both were guilty
Of certain crimes of omission
Yet, neither one
Of them ever looked
The other way
And signed me out.
Like they could have done.
But they didn't do that.
I don't know why.
It should not be a crime
To fall in the street.
Coming down,
I did not bump
Into anyone
Or even jostle
Anyone
Like what happens
On a subway
Every day
During rush hour.

AUGUST 6

The words that stood
On your tongue
For a little while
What did they mean?
You whittle away at them
Will nothing be summoned forth
The driftwood collected
From your trip north to Nova Scotia
Will all of the pieces be transformed
Into viable sea creatures?
The artist as a renunciate of dreams
What does she see happening
When the world wakes up
From its foolhardy reverie?
Can shop windows
Be replaced?
Can lives be returned?
Can the grace notes
And demi-quavers be restored
Or do the lives of musicians
Hang the balance?
Broken, can a pearl necklace
Restring its wand of purpose?.

On my sixty-seventh birthday
I grabbed the inside
Of an open car window
And hung on tightly
While the car was still moving.
It all might have presaged a warning
Eventually, when the car cooled to a stop.
In fact, the rejoinder
Might have been too fast in coming.
What are you doing here?
You're not supposed
To be predisposed
To slipping down this way.
As a displaced citizen
And as a ward of the state,
It's too late to reverse
The flow of the old tidal waters.
We'll give your guardian
Spirit friend twenty dollars a month.
For keeping you under wraps and lock and key.
That should be enough to do the trick.
That should have taken care of the predisposition
You have for taking on fits. And there you have it!

But you are my mother and father, aren't you?
Besides, isn't this my birthday. If you would only ask:
I'll have cake and ice cream with you.

We might spend the rest of the day

Together for a change.

As a matter of course,

Please go home.

That's your lot in life.

You have chosen

Everything that has happened as it has done.

Even getting born?

I chose that too, Mom?

As a bad dog kind of a thing

Please go home. That I will

And act totally content.

AUGUST 8

She sees a friend
At the supermarket
And throws her arms
Around his waist.
She cries.
He says:
Don't carry on so!
Here, let me help you
With the shopping and all.
She has three boxes
Of Weetabix
As well as cheerios.
Neither have mask,
Not even a couple of masks
Hanging from the cart
As surreal waivers
For their obvious states as oblivion.
When asked about what happens,
While the fur flies,
Voices in unison,
Mimic a reply:
Wearing a mask
Simply does not flow
With our degrees
Of consciousness

AUGUST 9

If chance favors
The prepared mind,
Chance and accident
Are each part of primeval chaos.
How can we make the best
Of the trickster in the doorway?
How can I steal butter
When everything in the house
Is mine and yours
Belongs to us as hierophants.
A baby's face was
Covered with flies.
Seeing this happening,
The parents proclaimed:
This was a very good way of god
Preventing something worse
From happening,
We can brush the flies off,
They come again.
We have no desire
To be lonely
For the myriad creatures
Coming to greet us in this world.

Can you recognize
Your own footsteps?
When slipping into a reverie
You don't mind wearing the mask
Of a doctor of consciousness.
It is just you haven't a clue
As to what an oracle book
Can mean when you have lost
All sense of balance.

Nothing you do will change
The world. Exposed,
The warrior still holds
Hunting knives.
The girl still holds a doll
Swans still somehow
Weave a meadow
Of shadows on a lake.
A thimble still holds
A bit of thread at bay.
A fretful child still cries
The cradle still holds the sound.
The paper holds indelible ink.

With a man like this in the room,
My child is not safe.
How did the man get in here anyway?
I never invited him in.
Are you crazy?
I would never think of doing that.
I am just the night clerk
Or even the day clerk
Supposedly working a shift
At the front desk.
Why is it in a season
Of scorching flames,
Dissolute, full of regret,
Full of anger and despair?
How is it that cold air
Can break into summer
So suddenly as passionately
As a whirlwind or a snowstorm?
With all that is happening,
Courtesy of the kindest
Inhabitants in the world
Living ever so happily
In their summer cave,
Isn't that crazy
To contemplate
Without going and getting
An immediate haircut?

August 13

Turn daylight
Upside down
Pull in midnight
By the next to nothing
Crescent moon.
If the indelible ink of karma
Won't rub off.
Those garbed
In prophecy's hastily put-together
Impromptu garment
Gleaned from the apocalyptic
Nickel and Dime
Will always spill the beans
To anyone who will in turn do the same again
Even at the *Holiday Thrift*
Whose members thrive across the street.

August 14

Barefoot and in vain, barefoot and derelict,
I followed you in vain, in rain sleet, and snow.
I was unaware that your teacher, such as he was,
Had gone and cursed me for a while.
No matter what happened, though god
Chided me for the road I traveled.
Nothing could stop in my tracks.
By the time I reached
The other side of the pond,
You had gone elsewhere.
I was in shock. You had shacked
Up with someone else.
Looking down from the balcony
Of lost loves, I want to know
Why when I sprinted past the Golden Gate,
Already, IU had dragged my heels. Perhaps, it is better to leave
Ostrich eggs alone under a park bench.
I often wonder what kind of a bloke you went with
Ending up in the haunted region of Wales, Aberystwyth.

Just look at you!
Aren't you the family man?
Spin me another yarn!
I've wanted to make
An animated film
For centuries.
About the green knight
From New Mexico,
About *Canary Portals,*
About *Meeting Grandmother Bird.*
I even dreamt of
A Chorale for Several Voices.
So many plans I had,
Had I only met the man!

AUGUST 16

About the narrator.

He is a much needed literary device for plays.

Yet, in real life drama, he hasn't a leg to stand on.

Nothing he did made any sense.

He already sold me out from under

A dozen web sites surrendered

Most of my works to him.

I am a dispute resolution

Mediator and I know

What I am talking about.

Having formed a psychic trade union,

When the bridge went down,

Everyone ran for their lives.

There was nothing further

Anyone could do about Boulder.

AUGUST 17

The jazz pianist knows how to play the piano perfectly,
And yet, this year, off set, he woke up and drowned.
Maintaining a supercilious interest
In the cause of the underdog,
Why did he lease his soul
To the cause of exclusionary rights of those
Who would abandon him?
Why did he drown? Did he really drown?
Is the need to act the part of a guardian angel
A royal rarity in this part of town?
Certain people won't wear mink coats.
Yet, they will walk beside
Rare specimens of lynxes,
Not detained from the forest by those hiding bejeweled leashes.
Meanwhile, most sleuthing investigators fail to uncover
The causes of numerous accidents
Occurring among circus barkers
Or among small time chivalrous yet rivalrous carnivals.
Why do animal trainers often get devoured by the media?
Or, by those whom they consider prodigious
Members of their so-called extended family?

Insofar as it is not fair for anyone
Not even a Sufi fakir, has been known to drown in the
melancholic waves of ocean.
Why did that rishi succumb to death by drowning?
In antiquated editions of his soul.
It does not matter overmuch,
The details of what actually transpired are mysterious.
Even if we sometimes drew near him
Without fearing the outreach of the community bowl
Of gazpacho soup,
Or even shared an imported tin of sardines
With baked beans for dinner,
From here on in, I reckon,
Having drawn down the same conclusions
As those thoroughly schooled in what rankled this Sufi most
Was this:
The boast of old wounds from childhood:
Revealed, reviled, exiled, yet never released.
As when as a light not fully snuffed out or extinguished
In beams of sunlight suddenly expires.
In any case of immutable drowning, at least,
The force is the one holding the final conversation.

AUGUST 19

Cats drowse
In marigold fields
Where sunlight's fitful
Countenance
Closes down their eyes
To silvered slits.
Bejeweled though those crepuscular eyes,
Before the approach of the evening star
On standby, you watch as the cats crawl back
Into the nocturnal darkness of their fearsome caves.
Why forgo giving you that final wayward glance?
They affirm the world betrays nothing of what they believe
What exists as circumstantial evidence.
Why grieve a jilted lover who is just the same?

This professor was a first-rate specimen
And absolutely the most incredible teacher.
He laughed when I sat down to play the piano.
He said the black and white keys
Part of a recessive gene. Eying me
As an antediluvian throwback
Drawn down from some wayward dynasty,
He praised my poetry as evidence
Of my piety. He did not realize
I flunked out of Mayhem University
And performed the Transylvanian shuffle
In an out of the way prison.
When ants began
Crawling into my eyes, he penned a poem
Called *A Lament For the Last Praying Mantis*.

AUGUST 21

Whenever I hear malicious gossip,
I know nothing has changed in the universe.
I want to lie down, have a breakdown, surrender,
Go home to the heavenly host and put my entire life on hold,
Or, at least, on a bit of an extracurricular lockdown.
Without my sister whispering in my father's ear,
Half-time every year, beneath a generous primrose-
Dotted umbrella offering ample and variegated shade,
I yearn to live on a beach found only in Rabat or in Tangier,
In a place where people sip sarsaparilla-tainted tea all day.
Dreaming beneath the moon's glimmering corona,
I want to skip a bright fandango equitable and suitable
For Brigands addicted to parachutes and daring,
Liminal, high-wire escapades.
I want to zero in on a heron's heroic and quiet meditation.
After trading in my tarot cards and repeatedly
Playing the violin, off key, since I need to forgo the imminent
Birth of a multi-modal eventual and virtual conscience,
Evidencing the need for multi-level carparks,
What about the need for the direct ambiance
Of an ambidextrous and aboriginal dreaming?
At present, I'm certain I'm not being followed by any class
Of monastic followers though,
I may be gifted with a virtual angelic audience,
What's inconvenient, though,
My heart pulsating among the frequent rewinds and reruns
Of ghostbuster movies.

Losing my purse at the carnival,
Losing my purse to my sister,
My daughters, as well as my brother,
What is there to live for?
Certainly not gold.
My birthday is a travesty
Of justice, but I am grateful
For a kitchen table bedecked with linoleum
Underfoot. How does one inhabit
The Garden of Eden, part-time,
And also work for an international Icelandic airline?

I believe a lot of people after spending
A lot of time walking in circles
Chasing after oracles, find they tire very easily.
How costly the price of beauty treatments, tummy tucking,
Eyebrow tattooing and so forth, and so on.
A fortnight ago, when I returned from my journey
To and from Alcatraz, I thought the plane, -
After rotating metallic wings,
Obediently surrendering to the dictates of tourist brochures,
After rendering up curbside service and
Offering a little breathing space,
I thought the plane would actually cut to the chase,
Obediently surrendering to the completion
Of its extracurricular excursion rate.
Perhaps, now thing would s go smoothly?
Baby, what was the point of all this traveling?
Baby, at least,
I thought, you would try placing your head on my shoulder,
A little while longer. Of course,
I had no reason to believe or disbelieve the psychics.
According to them, you would never bring back my Strad,
The one you'd borrowed
And promised to return to me so many years ago in Vladivostok.
I expected a least a ham and cheese sandwich
In return for all my kindly efforts.
After all, I had gone barefoot and had worn
The same dress for ten days,

All things being equal, wouldn't you know it,
After a lot of turbulence,
Since the entire journey was long, arduous and bold,
Not in a thousand years,
Did I ever imagine your Professor X would blame me
For your penultimate betrayal?
As well as your cowardly refusal to be named in a lawsuit?
I gave you everything I had.
I mean I'd never slept with anyone before.
Did he really believe I robbed the cradle?
What about his wife? As for me, only twenty-nine, and,
As for you. having twenty-five solid years
Tucked under your belt, I came to believe your professor
Was in favor of off-track betting.
Did he really think I needed a shrink?
Once situated at Angie's Bird Song & Fairy Kingdom Restaurant
In the way of some kind of a displaced suzerain
Or sultan in exile, in my wildest dreams
Never did I see, Professor X would ever set about
Ordering the entire staff of waitresses around?
Did he sense something about their humble backgrounds,
When they the performers
Hadn't a clue as to what was actually going on?
Perhaps. the whole thing, indicative
Of the transmigration of warring souls including
Transference and counter-transference.
Your professor never asked me nor did he appear
To ever want to know
Why I drilled little holes in my earlobes and preferred
Drinking herbal tea instead of coffee.
How could I estimate, he'd gone and memorized
Over a thousand sutras in Sanskrit?
Long since whenever, therefore,

He'd been declared a local surfing agent
And even some kind of saintly event
As evidenced in his own home town of Duluth?

What death will do is something none of us can easily do,
So, we might as well repair to our houses on lockdown.
Not even when told we are too old to protest, do we protest.
So, when a robber leaves his adobe hut to go rob an inn-keeper,
When a horse breaks from a coral and clears a fence,
When the gorgon's head
Crops up again in the kingdom, all too soon Death leaves people
To puzzle at the simple quilts of guilt, apathy, longing,
Ambition, & the spilt milk of ambition.
If it were not so, why would an eagle refuse to eat Zeus's liver?
Why was the God Attis ever hung from a pine-tree in Sumer?
Why did Odin agree
To hang down from the world ash tree for over nine nights?
Your hearth song may be the only sign of an alliance
With the goddess of poetry and music,
But whatever happens, we must forget the timeless labyrinth,
The bardo
Marked only by hand-wringing sighs of those whose limbs
Outstretched on the couch of analysis
For the next incarnation as a fish.

AUGUST 25

Come skate upon thin ice
Until it melts
Sigh until tears
Make you turn in
Your pilot's license
Once and for all
When a horse clears a fence
He allows you
To understand freedom
In freedom's name.
Balancing within an urn
Until ash plant spill its fire,
Love is no more until blood
Begs a different direction home.
When I look up from my book,
The stars are awash
In dismemberment of stone and mercury.
If the way has always been this clear,
Before the face of a thousand otherworldly eyes,
Can the honeycomb master fear?

AUGUST 26

To conquer fear
You need audacity
Or a peacock to fly
Straight towards the center of your soul-eye.
When your heart calls out to you
And each one of your crimes is revealed
In the way of a small cricket
Caught in a humble leaf-thicket, thorn and briar-filled,
When jarred and jilted mid-sentence,
While still intent upon protesting his innocence,
Why not offer nothing but good in return for evil?

August 27

Angels can be considered a hoax,

Emerging from a humble winking fire,

What of the calendars of their unremembered lives?

Like anyone else, when called upon a carpet,

Whether their remarkable wings are snipped,

Like spindrift, their songs remain light-filled and unbroken.

So, have mercy upon them!

Sighing. as they die a thousand deaths

Undetected, few have reached their final home.

Closer to the harmonic source of the crystal kingdom,

Far more easily they die, than you or I.

AUGUST 28

In the pit of my stomach: fear.
Unless you stop,
I cannot waltz long enough.
My dress is floor-length
Stars too near
To mask confession's hemisphere.
The noise of the world,
Maddening in cases
Of mistaken identity
Like this.

AUGUST 29

Pleasure is akin
To this maddening
Wakefulness.
Heavy-lidded,
Some wings of sound.
Moths alone
Can save me
From myself.
Inside my shoe,
A grasshopper,
A cricket waits.
All year. I lived
In the simple
Grip of death.
I know what
Freedom is for.
Goose-bumps.

AUGUST 30

If the dead command
What I am to become
I don't know why.
I have written
On rice paper
On my bed sheets.
On all fours
I have crawled
Past many streets
All the way to the foot of the temple
I have looked deeply into a lake of blood.
You cannot tell me I have not tasted
Wisdom's knowledge

AUGUST 31

She is as near-sighted as she once was before.
We cannot go back into the doctor.
We were charged just one hundred dollars
For a bottle of vitamin C tablets.
A small bug is crawling over my hand.
Tell me all the pigeons cooing on the roof
Are unenlightened.

September

Come Autumn and Trees Are

Heart-Broken

September 1

Corner the dragon, as a would-be possessor
Of ordinary episodic interludes of trauma.
If he does not spell out all the details
Of his next, true-to-life. bloodcurdling, horror novel.
Too bad, there's certainly an expiration date
On everything, even on flashlights from libraries
Lighting up the cosmos for a second.
Everything that transpires and takes place between us
Hearsay of course. Nothing is to be
Repeated except in confidence
Because of the necessity
Of protecting anonymity's news hour anchors.
Meanwhile, the dragon's mouth remains closed.
In all likelihood, he swears he knows nothing of meteors
Not even the one that blew out all the windows in Novosibirsk
He's not familiar with that fire-filled tumbleweed or evil deeds.
Even when Mary was in the habit
Of wearing one embroidered peasant blouse,
That suited her figure perfectly,
He was never even allowed or permitted
To see eye to eye with you.
He even stopped the interview, mid-sentence.
He pretends ignorance
Beneath his dignity
That which you're talking about
From way back, he learned to lie.
If he's the one wearing a baseball cap

Backwards and sometimes forwards
Hasn't he always been a Mensa member
Even from the age of five years.
Your money or your life,
He must be your man.
Your man from the dreamtime
The man who drops a red feather
From a flicker or a cardinal
A feather meant for his bride.

SEPTEMBER 2

Don't sit too close to me. please
Misfortune may get in the way
There's no turning back
No inkling of a relationship of any kind,
To those persons, living or dead.
Once you've left
The skating rink,
Once you've left a lake, swan-filled, or not
It is often impossible to prevent
Leg-warmers from unraveling
And leaving your leg unprotected
Vulnerable, your life misinterpreted
Before your leg performs
As part of the last signatory party
To a swift, fast-moving glissade
The dance of pas de *bourree*
Returning sheets of thin ice to god.

SEPTEMBER 3

Such an easy piece and picture
Of surreal conjectural knowledge for him.
What kind of a news hour item was this anyway?
He pictures me in the grip
Of some surreal mystery story.
I am not quite the main character,
Instead, he thinks like a contortionist or a midget
Emerging from a Tom Thumb wedding cake,
He has been gifted
With some kind of supernatural talent
Befitting no one else but a country gentleman.
Meanwhile, I am dependent on someone else
I have no driver and no ring on my left hand.
I have no earrings
No poetry in the offing
I am a heron balancing
On wisdom's lake.
If you saw someone
Deliberately, defiantly,
Murdered in the way
He definitely did,
In that offhand counterfeit moment
In which he states I did not see anything
And I am not responsible for witnessing anything
Out of the way
It is better to deny
Being a lawyer and affirm in a make-believe

Statement of super hyper-realism

Everything is hearsay

Nothing worth

Remembering

Save on the bay foxglove

Sprouting from beneath a park bridge

Nothing caught sight of

Except that which was glimpsed

In an out of the way place,

Sprouting after dark. Meanwhile,

Kafka's after-shave lotion

Sporting such a lovely scent,

You'd think the air

Perfumed with lovely

Jasmine flowers

After all,

When, in keeping with the suspense of the novel,

Nothing of the kind was meant.

The plum tree falls to the ground.

Autumnal leaves were too close to it.

The bark weeping

Over the disturbance.

The wounding of spectacular plums?

SEPTEMBER 4

A book of the soul
Far too difficult to read.
She keeps telling me not my karma
The celebrity status of elves.
Not my karma the successful journey
To the Himalayas.
Not my karma the darkening
Of oleander flowers
Encircling a forgotten tomb.
Must I wait for customers
All day in a museum
Meant for liars
Filled with unutterable
Syllables of balderdash?

Once in a while I call her.
She is elderly and usually a bit lonely.
From the beginning of time,
I was fearful our friendship would founder.
One day, when I call, she says I am with my lover
And cannot be disturbed, sorry!
Tethered wings are often filled with thorns.
For years, I have waited for the gardener
The only problem is I pay him for snipping
My roses. In spring, people talk about
Going to the opera. I am of the opinion
Heavy-lidded clouds must then unpin
My engagement with him. In spring,
I may not ever see him again.

I want to write leaping poetry
And confront a flying fish
A flying squirrel
A lynx leaping from a branch
A kite drowning in air
Raven thought he could steal
Fishing bait and that he could get away with that
Still to maintain a schedule of flying through the air
As he were a parasol-dancer on a trapeze
With a net to catch him if he fell along the way.
As for journeys flying to and from a given destination
I would defer first to prophecy's vertiginous nightmare.
Before defining my journey home.

September 7

We met in the Denver train station.

The voice echoes in there as if a wounding

Had taken the place of the voice itself

Seeking out a place to land, a train to catch.

You sat on a bench and spoke and I watched

As your whisper echoed, repeating itself ten times

Bouncing all over outer the accouterments

Of outer space.

The next time I came to Denver

You were gone.

The next month they tore down the station.

Why praise Apollo's shoulder?
A quiver of arrows grace
His musical acumen and prowess.
But the chiseled grace of a marble statue
Surpasses any paean I might pen.
If I have a chance visit Delos,
Without a tourist manual
How will I know how to greet him?
What to say to him?
Horace owns a Sabine villa.
Meanwhile, the half-clad lad from Santorini,
He knows what to do.
Bring along lyre and strum
On the Peloponnesian strings
Until the ocean levels our wits to glass,
Dipping our tunics,
A class of Stygian blue.

SEPTEMBER 9

Hobble the ubiquitous horse
That wants to know how to run away
Already bridled and harnessed
It makes no difference
To the witless impulse
No matter what, in a few minutes,
He'll clear the fence.
Confine the girl to her room
The girl effortlessly trying
To borrow a set of jangling keys,
Keys to her ubiquitous family sedan
Later on, will you be the one taking notice?
Logging in & pulling a mystery school's all-nighter?
Divorce has taken its toll making a slight subdivision
Between shrimp boats and their teenage fisher folk.
The best of show among the sum total
Among the draw of superlative reggae tunes,
The girl already knows which bodies are the softest.
In a drought, a creek inhibits its speckled pebbles
Most of the time. When stones ground down to sand,
An hour glass may delay its gravity's pull.
What's deemed as mostly beautiful by some,
Not dutiful enough. As for those who love
Playing a game of tiddlywinks after dark,
Why pity the unseen karmic effects of love?
Why not go about worshipping art?

September 10

When little May sings the opening lines
Of her birthday rant, chaos follows.
Can't she see she's the only one
Singing happy birthday alone, and out of tune?
Her crooning significantly differs
From the chanted demi-quavers and rules
Of the pentatonic scale and is totally off-key.
One day, when no one was listening
She dared consult a tuning fork.
Out of greed, is deceit spawned among
The souls of ignominious singers?
Among silvered chrysanthemum leaves,
Pain only shatters darkness. When the moon drops
Down among the feathered grasses of a field,
Drowning in a keening wind
These two move up
When music misunderstood,
When the body breaks down its sacrament of flesh
In a country of exile,
Silence learns the unbending of its iron tongue.
I want to leave everything of this world behind
Praying in a language of beloved deliverance
Hummingbirds have now decided to unwind
Unpacking any chance of losing of severance pay.

September 11

Until music entered into the raging
Flight of his toes,
He did not know
What was happening to the rest of his body nor to the building.
So, the story goes that was endless, boundless, not a hoax
Instead an inimitable and mammoth disaster, relentless
Resonating, shattering all consideration of sensibility and reason
Ricocheting from the crow's nest.mo
On this date, the world was no more.
Or that is what it seemed.
So terrifying today a monument exists
For all those human souls who perished
Admonishing a compassionate god
For having lost their lives.
When it was not his fault, not really.

September 12

I told the waiter.
I told the waitress.
How can it be
I am held responsible
For what this man does
Or does not do.
The one whom I know best,
His wife, she has departed
From this world.
Only as his wife's friend
Was where I came in
That did not mean
I ever understood
The meaning of life
What consort means
Or driving a car so fast.
Traffic lights no more have color.
Even when the car cooled to a stop,
It barely slithered into position
On a road already seething
With a rumor of pontifical angels.
Still I do not know
What I am talking about.
Besides I am not a medium
All I know, for a while,
He was reading
A book of Rilke's

For one hundred days.

But that was not enough for him

I don't know which angel

He was on when his dead wife descended.

And then this was when he was transformed.

SEPTEMBER 13

Now his clothes carried
A perfume of love, all tweedy-like
Sent down from heaven
Sent down from heaven
Straight from the arms
Of his dead wife.

September 14

Of course, she was
Not really dead.
Do you really
Believe she was
Dead I mean.
Do you believe
In death. I know
It is wholly possible
To keep on thinking
Multiplying the possibilities
For ways of thinking about death
Even if you do or do not
Believe in the resurrection
Of the holy spirit
And are of several minds
About what to think
And why you think the way
You do you might stop and pause
And take a breather
You could still start believing
In death almost as a sample
Of a real or unreal person.
That's what I think anyway.
The bluest soul
Is not really blue.
Perhaps it's green with envy,
But that form of cancer

We will not go into
Not at this juncture.
Anyway, we are talking
About something else
In this poem.
Something critics
May not understand
Or cast aspersions upon.

SEPTEMBER 15

Like I said. I knew her
For a very long time
I knew her on earth.
And yes, she was a lovely woman
Considered the same
By all those people
Who knew her like I did
Chancing betimes to meet her
On the meandering path
To wherever it was
She and they
Might be on
In the process
Of going their way
Without any sign or excuse
Of succumbing to loathsome detour
Such as the times when they
Were both going to work
Or out and about to purchase
Something in the shops
Or to buy a new dress
Or something earth-shattering
Of that variety.

In fact, in truth,
A blinkered horse
Might froth
At the mouth
Beginning to break his harness
With unbridled acts of kindness
Breaking ranks with idleness
Just to catch sight
Of the beauty of this woman
On her telepathic journey
To god knows where
But you know better-
Upstairs

SEPTEMBER 17

That's the way it was
And that's the way she was
Her spirit playfully
Dancing around her.
On some occasions
She was even seen wearing
A handsome and winsome riding jacket
Designed by Kanga of Kensington Gardens.

SEPTEMBER 18

Yes, she was a wise woman.
Meanwhile, as for her husband
He continued reading Rilke.
He read the book
Of his dead wife's angels.
But then his soul
Went into revolt.

And then he stopped
He didn't approve
Anymore of continuing
To read the book of her body's angels.
At that moment, when his dead wife
Came alive and entered his body.
Butter began melting
Beneath the lilting tongue
Of a medium who also read
The book of his dead wife's body
But that was not enough.

At that point, suddenly,
What happened?
Wouldn't you know it,
Without reasonable
Or virtual grain or gram of explanation
Or expectation,
He did what most humans do
Even in a novel
It might be considered
Inconceivable or incredible
What he did
He fell in love.

SEPTEMBER 21

Not with the medium

Not with a waitress

Not with his dead wife's friend.

Instead, he fell in love with another woman

Who had never met his dead wife at all

Even though they lived

In the same apartment block for years

And may have passed each other

Every morning according to an inner calendar

And still they may not have realized

The possibility of two souls

Interfacing likes vines of ivy on a garden wall.

Intertwining for eternity's sweet sake

Or at least as long

As posterity would allow them so to do

Now the new woman appearing on the map
Let's call her, Althea,
Was a woman who lived in exile
A woman who had been banished
From a Transylvanian mountain kingdom.
If she was beautiful
Her beauty might have been called
Into question
For as a wise woman and a crone
As the fairest woman
In a land of plenty
Her spirit familiar
And very accustomed
To dancing a rambunctious
And volatile maypole dance
Around the man's
Dead wife and yes
Such dancing continuing on to the point
Well and good, enough so you might think
And you might assume and you might suppose
The man's dead wife had actually known her
Or had been her best friend during the course
Of both of their lives. Doubtless it was
Countless times, she had had
Several of those.

September 23

Be that as it may,
In this regard, this certainly
Was not the case, though.
This is because and since
In real life
They had never met in person.
It does not matter.
It cannot matter now
I suppose it cannot
Because I mean
Whatever transpires
Whatever happens
Proof positive
Life as we know it
Is bound to unravel
The way it does
Knit one pearl one
Has always been my credo
As fate decrees the fate
Of the human race
And every hair on the head
Of mankind and womankind
And wunderkinds
Well-accounted, numerous times
And surely even unto and until
The developing strands engaging in
The devolvement of the next life

If that is what you believe
And you are not deceived
By the strictures accruing
To the parameters and precincts
Of the monolithic culture.

September 24

It just all goes to show
That to all ways of thinking
When I sit right down
And begin to take stock of my life
And all that happened and transpired
Things like this rarely happen
But sometimes they do happen.
And I am not a medium
So, I do not know
Anything.
But I am well-apprised
As to the fact his dead wife
Because she has travelled
Through the hole in the sky
That is heaven
Must know everything
Because she is a wise woman
And she has been upstairs
Reading the book of her body
And Rilke and the books of the angels
That is totally fair for all those seeking justice
Within the golden pages of medieval romances.

September 25

Even now up in heaven
As things stand to be foretold
Still and all, plenty of surprises
Are unfolding as we speak
In the way of ravens scattering
Over the length and breadth
Of this land and the kingdom
Of incredulity where this story
Unfolded and was deconstructed,
Week after week after week.

Every night we hear
The cat's meow.
We assume it is a cat.
But we're not sure.
We eat berries
At midnight
That's when we
Give the cat the slip.

SEPTEMBER 27

My name is Lucy White
She said.
I am allowed
To do my knitting
If I so choose.
I was on the bus that day
On my way to school
When my sister died.
Afterward, people
Kindly told me where to go.
When the sun rose,
When the sun set,
I knew it not.
The knots in my hair
Thickened. I could
Not run a comb
Anywhere
Near my head.
Just like my daddy
Always said:
We were two peas
In a pod.
Now she is dead.

I walk the roads
To keep myself awake.
To have been the last person
To have gone about
Visiting
What is left of this world?
Is that all that the parabola
Of transcendence is about?
Left living within the confines
On the planetary surround
Thriving on pleasure
And displeasure's stranglehold,
Who is fooling the ones that are left?
He hassles me for money,
He hassles me for gold.
Far too many times
For my liking,
He hassles me for his cigarettes.
This is the way
He bothers
To make a living.
Nothing matters overmuch
Except money.
Frightened, I don't want
To make myself ill
Over his wrong-doing.
Longing

For a better way of life,
When it is all over,
I want to know
I moved some people.
When you see a hawk
Rising
From meadow hedgerow,
I want you to know
It is my wings reaching
Touching the blazing persimmon
Of what is left of the moon's shadow.

SEPTEMBER 29

Wine clouds my grief.
Coming back into this life,
Do I want to continue?
My rising to the pond's surface
Under duress
Is the place for
Trading war stories.
Shall I pretend these are our last birds ever heard on earth,
Their wings, stirring, these birds,
Singing in the crosshairs of moonlight?

SEPTEMBER 30

Whale calves
Singing underwater.
I hear their songs
I know life above ground
Matters much less than before.
Arthritis in my knees.

October

The Deeper the Vessel,
the Greater the Wine

As for the man
Who died,
One-size-fits-all,
At the yoga institute
In Duluth.
Harold, yes, he's gone
The poor man is gone
To a far better place.
Let us consider
What happens in Duluth
When after a new baby is born,
One profits from
Multiple greetings.
Off stage,
Someone who knows
All the riddles and mysteries of birth
Is heard proclaiming in increments:
One for joy!
Two for a girl!
Three for a boy!
Mouthing suitable
Soothing words,
Will take care
Of the bewildered mind
The torment of the soul
Cannot forestall
Innate proclivity towards wine.

OCTOBER 2

Greet the autumnal tree
With a blessing.
Watch as russet leaves
One by one, are clocking
Shorter
Daylight hours.
Turning to gold,
Every leaf,
Dying to be reborn
As jackdaw and wren
Celebrate
Your birthday.

OCTOBER 3

The devil made me do it.
Is that what people say
Suddenly becoming
Disconsolate while lamenting
All that has transpired
Among history's malcontents?
Blame it on the incumbent,
Blame it on the lost soul society,
Blame it on the people who have no ankles.
Why else should the sun blacken?
As god is busy witnessing a moon inciting to riot
Multiple shadow players, do his eyes fill with tears?
Seen as difficult dervish followers,
If a cockroach and a cricket are caught in a dispute
Just for brandishing a knife in a public place?
Who questions the facts of the case?
By definition, both are innocent creatures.
For the blade had always been sheathed.
Deprived of any evil & criminal offense,
Fearing a tawdry uprising of some kind,
To some degree, if Father Sky glimpsed willing
Thickening the air with deceit of dark clouds
Lanced with grimace of lightning flash
If the blindly partisan reveal under Biblical oath,
Every last secret and hidden blind decree,
How will things evolve
Not in god's good time as far as I can see.

Under relentless cross-examination,
We expect what's true is absolutely full proof.
Unless rage chosen as the final poison
Killing you as naturally as a decree
Or, as a divine word offered
Kindly before a sword.

October 4

She said: everyone knows
What love is when we sit together.
The entire room changes.
Every molecule dances
That ever had a body.
Even the sound of the wind
Is different. The wind
That never stops blowing
Rejoices and makes the pine
Trees dance, too. What other point
To being in love ever existed.
No one can explain what happens
When he is with me. The entire
Coffee shop could close down
But we would still sit hand in hand
As if ghosts of another time.

Known as a poet,
Since he is not,
He says
In my youth,
I must have forgotten
How to rime.
Pretending to be
Rather hard of hearing,
She says something like
I never heard what happens next
In this compassionate back story.
Is this nothing but a lament?
After a brood of guinea hens
Come lallygagging through a field.
Strange isn't it,
The leaving of indelible
Voice-prints behind
Among miraculous dahlias,
Left trembling with vertigo?
Now back to what she says.
She says: I feel invisible wings
Brushing past my shoulder.
Later, everything changes
When she says:
Knowing you are an angel,
That should be enough
To make you want to sing

The gospel according

To the fear of falling

In love. Later, he says:

Just to hear Martha

Beating a brass bowl

With a stick is enough.

I never asked for so much

As the touch of a knife

A flashflood, or explosions

Of grief in my life.

For lone minute,

She allows herself

To look into the sun.

That's just the ordinariness

Coming out of you. Because

You haven't a clue as to how to go on.

Following the line of flat country

With her hand, she entertains the notion:

Nothing is written in stone.

I can imagine kingfishers and curlews

Crying out as leaping sparks fly out

From behind my head.

He says: I'm not sure why I came to earth.

You know I have another wife in Mexico.

A moose meditates and then walks out of lake

As if nothing has happened.

The moon hovers over a dead man's hut.

I never asked to be loved in quite this way.

OCTOBER 6

Maybe you were someone
I never knew or thought I knew.
Though you left your coat
On the coat rack, a sign
Of your return, not forthcoming.
Words catch in my throat.
Once having glimpsed heaven,
It makes no sense to marry Jack.
As to how many souls have passed over
Since your departure, the tectonic plates have moved.
If omnipotent cries of the Canadian geese
Persistent as a poor child crying in his sleep
Or more like a wise man crying into his beard,
Fallen to ruin, the half-moons of your nails
Cannot be those of a monk who recalls the light as an ally.
I promise I will act more obedient in future
And move to the coast.
Relatives cannot go on stealing
Every last one of my tennis shoes.

OCTOBER 7

Because I stumble over words,
Does that mean I am slow?

The cat has gone away.
We have to think circus
And circus barker.
We have to think
Wounds made visible
On a dog. A rabbit
Snatched from a lair.
A coyote barking
Off the ear of a watch dog.
A raven cawing
Because he stole
Bait meant for fishing.
A gazelle not meeting
His appointment
With leaping.
We have to think autumn
A purse made out of a sow's ear.
Barely are there
Enough ghosts to talk
About the absence.
On the cellphone
A female voice howls:
Why did he have to die?
At least he was not alone.

OCTOBER 9

We don't know
What to believe.
Cooking up larger than life charts
A map making man can prove
Flying to and from a gloved hand,
A falcon will return
Singing the beards
Of starving prophets?
As a winged falcon
Subsumes currents and cross currents
With his wings,
The map maker has been made a signatory
To a contract: render those maps
Accessible. Render them as beautiful
As Turkish rug designs.
There's a charge
For the sum total cost of these charts.
Only for a short time,
Will we put that aside
In favor of eying the wings of comets,
Though he has factored in
Many points referring
To divination's learning,
What do the dead care?
They are out of earshot.
It is becoming
Increasingly difficult

To transcribe the notes
Of the young girl
Sitting at the Saint Jude Café.
Though the map-maker has extended
The limits of the imagination
The latter is only
An imagined shell.
While iambs and trochees
Inhabit the world of poetry
Flickering in the wind,
Without a metronome
While unlit cadences
Of leaves multiply
Reinventing shadows,
There comes a point
When we must consider
We cannot comfort
The dark journey of the map-maker.
Like everyone else
He just wants a coin in his pocket.
Something else
Dire is occurring.
People are dying.
Has the map-maker
Forgotten
The river takes
Everything
To the delta?
Blurt out the truth
Don't let the truth
Stay in your head,
Not for another minute.

OCTOBER 10

How could I have missed you?
That would be considered impossible.
In the same town
Where synchronicity plays
Such an important part
Within the bright core of our reckoning
Where these things are neither fables nor acts of contrition.
Rather they are blood-curdling cries.

In the same town where
Several women with whom
I am unfamiliar conserve apricots and peaches
And pigs' trotters in jam jars on the sly,
While flickering candles
Snuffed out, agree to expire,
As part of his agreement with the stars,
Hermit-like, the man upstairs
Stays glued
To his computer all day.
Will Rome fall in one day?

Hand in hand
How can we go outside?
Small boned animals
May have thought
To take refuge in our bodies
But they could not.

The jewels that we wear
Are considered suicidal
Ornaments
Before a gleaming sun.

October 11

It hasn't happened yet.
We haven't found a leader.
Or have we?
We reach our hands
Into a pile of dead leaves
Rattlesnakes, a hornet's nest,
Warrior ants.
In the headlights
Of an approaching car
We see everything too late.
Our hands feel the touch
Of too late to save ourselves.
Restless in their stalls,
Horses paw the earth
Who needs an equine
Horse-hoof trimmer?
To bury a body underground
Seems such a waste.
Why forestall
Indictment
Of a shovel or a pickaxe?
At night, everyone
Must ask for the task
Of forgiveness
We kept asking
For news
From the other side.

Just let people know
The voice that cries
From the other side
Died of small pox
Not so long ago.

OCTOBER 12

You know how to honor this day
But other people do not.
They overturn the boat.
They loot storage bins
And warehouses.
Everyone knows the territory
By now.
If we were discovered,
Ask about Jamestown
The lost colony.
Why the people
Shifted has never been adequately explained.
Perhaps, members of the lost colony
Were not really lost at all.
My Mom told me
If I did ballet in Phoenix
I would end up
Starving and in a bad way
You know what happens when
You get lost in bedsitting community
Or starving in a Parisian garret.

OCTOBER 13

Don't talk to me
About being a poet.
After the appendix came out
You were gone.

Through the glass darkly
Simply does not apply to me.
Your ashes still warm
My impossible hands.
I thought I had you
But I lost you.
You slipped through
The fingers of the universe
The way in which
An ice boat lags
Behind a spirit
That has already
Knows where that place is
And the boat knows
About the conditions of ice
Still waiting for it.
If the veils are thin
They are still majestic.
Majestic is the suffering
Of all those who love,
Whose love is not returned
Or redeemed like a lost railway ticket.
If you follow the line of reasoning,
Blossoming along gooseberry bushes
Edging along living Cherokee Trails
Running north and south,
And a few other places,

I can make mention of,
But I won't,
Love never get you anywhere.

OCTOBER 15

I figured out
How to send you another poem
Written at lunch time.
I have a hunch about it
It just might do the trick.
Whoever dies first,
We can map out a palace of justice
A courthouse where
When the sky empties itself
Of all manner of color,
It may still let us both
Bury the hatchet
At precisely the same time,
All in god's time.
The empty spaces in the sky
Have filled all the empty places
Where people do not care to let you know
They do not even want to know
Whether you have window boxes
Filled with perennials.
Is it the same for you?
At Fort Winnetka,
I find it excruciating
To live between two worlds.
I am not sure they pack
Picnic lunches in heaven.

OCTOBER 16

I don't want to talk
About the big car
I packed all my belongings in it.
It broke down.
Year after year, I always have premonitions
About cars breaking down
Packed with all my belongings,
The car never made it up the mountain
For a fortnight, it lay on the side of the road
Like sheepherder's heavy,
Load, abandoned and derelict.
When the police towed it away
That very act of towing
Proved everything I said
About the way
We could never live together
It also proved to me I was crazy
For planting vague recollections
Of our several meetings
Going screaming among petunias
Screaming from window boxes,
Bathed in supernatural moonlight.

OCTOBER 17

When Sonia fed the chickens
She wasn't sure what she really
Wanted out of life.
Seeing old people get sick and die
Made her certain she never wanted
To stay with her grandmother again
And see the same thing happen to her
That happens to everyone in the entire world.
Her state of non-compliance made no sense.
But it was part of her dreams of becoming an artiste.
Under lamplight,
She dreamed she gave birth
To herself as an angel.
She did not believe in god.
God only wanted to make a fool out of her.
When a fox descended
Tackling three pullets at a time
She became convinced
She had to find out
Whether her conscience
Was listening to the messages
She was getting or not.
Pinned down by the stillborn routine
Of daily tasks, she soon asked
That creator let her cut to the chase
And escape immediately
To a Parisian landscape.

When she got to Paris,
She wore those cool
Criss-cross stockings.
When her traveling companion
Ditched her
In a Parisian Café,
For being less than décolleté
An old woman also a hunchback
Typical in those parts
Began watching her as she strolled
About in the market-place.
A meadow is as unpredictable
As bobolinks making an escape
From the jeweled eyes of a rattlesnake.
Averting her gaze
As long and as best she could,
She swore at the old woman,
Why lean
Against a wall,
When you are a child
Drowning in such a way
Each wave is a cormorant riding the moon
Is that the secret place inside your own heart,
A place might have called home?

OCTOBER 18

I lie in wait in burial clothes.
Call this a winding sheet
If you want. Waiting for war,
Asking for renumeration
Rehearsing all the details
About how much they've suffered
In the private catafalque of the courtyard
During the course of their lives
Warriors ants come in fully clothed,
Looking at the birds
Flying over head
Knowing full well
Because of their brightly colored plumage
Consciousness simply does not end up dead.
I list the way in which tiny threads knit together
All the pieces of my spine.
The softest places in my body
Are waiting for your hands
And for the bones to dissolve
Like the moon at mid-morning.
You have only to lie in wait
So long and someone will find out
The garden will admit one.
Lifetimes beget lifetimes.
A good tablecloth
Never covered an entire table
In a nonsensical restaurant of sorts.

Who really wants to stay as a part of this world
Long enough to glimpsed the details of the next life?

OCTOBER 19

The cat has a future
In a mock-up rendition of this life.
Absolved of any interest
Lying in a bankruptcy proceeding,
All she has to do is to confess
To a habit of over-grooming.

OCTOBER 20

More than anything
A man wanted his child
Out of a sleeping coma.
Any father would
Want the same.
Not a religious man,
Hadn't he heard of Padre Pio?
Yes, he had. So, he decided
To go to the Pittsburgh area
It was somewhere
Around in that district
Padre Pio's relics
Were held in a reliquary
By members of a church
Devoted to his grace of the holy one,
Taking Brenda's yellow shirt
He laid it on a relic
Belonging to the miraculous body
He prayed.
When he returned
To the hospital,
Father dressed his daughter
In Brenda's own yellow shirt
Now irradiated with
Padre Pio's reliquary energy.
The next day
Brenda woke up,

Wild with weeping,
Were father and mother,
An afternoon rain
Still plummeting,
A roller-coaster ride
For which
There has never been
Any ending.

October 21

Look around you and decide
Who is the most authentic
Most dependable
And blessed human being?
Decide which one of you
Is truly out of the woods.
All things being equal,
Do you praise the lover,
Or despise him to bring him
To an awareness of bliss?
Will he know how to manifest
What is best
For the masses?
You cannot claim him
As your friend
Unless the peach tree
Comes in with a fierce wind
Of autumnal blossoming.
Such blossoming, they were
Never within the provenance of spring.

Never has been any reason
For this type of fallout.
If you are able,
Collect yourself,
Convene your senses,
Take a sip of wine.
Prior to this existence,
Who were you then before?
Does this matter more or less
Or less and more.
Don't worry, in any event,
Trees were bound to flourish
On the forest floor
Growing pine cones
Even before your absence
Taken any notice of.
My mother told me
Most of the old fables
Existing in the old country
Were of a most practical
And useful nature. Follow them
If you follow them, you need
Not follow god and the angels.
After placing a hand gingerly
On the golden pages
Of old-world dictionary,
Acting as a *femme fatale type of Van Winkle*,

Translating out of a profligate game
Of Scrabble, that was found
Not to be all that difficult.
Not for those people who had no problem
Worshipping rightfully at Humility's blessed portal of alphabets
At the foot of the Mountain where
Master provided all the answers.

OCTOBER 23

Little Faith Hope Harding
Was one of a number of indigo children
Endowed with exceptional tendencies.
Except, in the past,
No children carried
The title: indigo children.
In an old photograph
She stands just four feet tall
Next to a pile of stones
Stacked up as twin portals
Serving as a testimony
To the veracity of her speeches
What a leaf stands to gain
From bole and bark of a tree,
Don't beggar Hope's litany
By loving the roots or the trunk
And despising bole or leaf
Prayerfully considered,
Each part of the tree
Must be revered equally,
Glimpsed as part
Of an entire majesty of heaven
This child must be made
To feel at home in her home
As no other human has ever been.

OCTOBER 24

As for the one who profits from prophecy
Which of these creatures' profits
The least endearing or everlasting?
What's more is it the kingdom of the rabbit,
The hare, or the wild-eyed raccoon?
Is the ferret, the weasel, or the mole?
Is it the deer or the curlew or the heron?
Or the sullen and loose-lipped moose you'd like to thank?
How would you like the terms of prophecy
Restored and served up?
To a gnat who would fly away? To a fish who would swallow
The truth and take it the bottom of the pond?
This puzzle is enough to confound the bearded sages.
Patiently waiting, they've been staring down the truth for ages.

Once there was a great poet who loved
Nothing better than to pen archaic verses
Embellishing the truth whenever plausible.
He had one problem, though,
Presenting himself as an imposter kind of a shadow-player,
He challenged a second poet to a duel.
What's worse to consider the dueling,
The bickering was never over.
It did not concern the accouterments of a woman
Or even a man; instead, it concerned a mock battle
Between two furious allies,
Jealousy and Greed. These had been close school chums of his.
Since the beginning of childhood, he failed to remain humble.
The first poet began telling the second poet he was soon to die,
The second imagined him entering into Gethsemane's Garden
Lopping off branches from the poet's sacred willow.
Seeing the potential for destruction, in an offhand remark
The second poet was quick to open with a humble reply:
All in god's time that is within the provenance of heaven.
No matter how gifted and talented they appear,
Poets know nothing.
The first poet responded in the way
Of a braggart's heart still pulsating.
Knucklehead, he said, I see no improvement in your writing.
You know I'm absolutely going to win.
The owl in a darkened forest
Beggars your spiritual investments in earnest.

The first poet went after the second poet repeatedly.

Much to my chagrin, I always keep my options open.

The second poet witnessed his would-be opponent with integrity.

Over a hastily arranged salmon dinner composed mostly of bones,

What was holding the second poet back came to light.

You've gained too much weight.

The kingdom of desire a lost cause,

The bullying poet told the second; that said, he quickly added.

How could you aspire to gaining any sort of meritocracy?

With that stammering stutter of yours, who'd take you seriously?

Aspiring to scale the mountains of civility is a wanton task.

For all those refusing the wearing of glamorous masks.

Humbled as you are by episodic bursts of sunlight,

I fail to see how in a month of Sundays

By not so much as one ounce,

You'll n'er grow any thinner

In hosting tonight's all-time winner.

That's the gist of what the first poet told the second.

The outcome of the duel is yet to be reviled or revealed.

OCTOBER 26

Hurdy-gurdy music plays outside an open window
Of a café. It is the same music that puts babies to sleep
And wakes up criminals and saints.
Someone plays the squeeze-box.
Please will someone gift me fifty cents!

OCTOBER 27

Clog-dancing brings me to my feet.
Washboards and castanets.
Drumming and playing the bones and the spoons.
In this café everyone has forgotten Covid.

October 28

We've flung open the doors to this café.
We've eaten outside all summer.
We've drunk wine from paper cups.
We've hugged people only elbow to elbow.
When do we relax our struggle?
The sun is still hot.
This is autumn.
Everyone says
Something worse is coming.

OCTOBER 29

There is a finality to a birthday
Before Halloween.
Words finally blew our lives apart.
Our friendship worth less than a sixpence,
That's what I think.

OCTOBER 30

Scolding never works.
People die in the valley.
People die in the city.
In the suburbs, the cemetery is an easy target
For interlopers, intruders, and trespassers.
Who gives a hoot about anyone else?
A man with a whole lot of statistics
Under his belt
Says absolutely nothing has ever been true.
Since when have we fact checked such memorabilia?
We should surrender our masks forthwith
And step over dead bodies in the street.
The Swedish experiment proved right:
When a lover exits from stage left,
No one should ever eat meat,
At least not in the spotlight.
The rules keep changing.
Shape-shifters keep on changing.
After darkness angelic saints
Come out of the woodwork
To proclaim the glory of god.

OCTOBER 31

No trick or treats this year.
Play music in the back yard
For the children.
Rewind all tapes. Fast forward.
Next year there'll be hobgoblins again.
My own sense of belonging
Compromised.
A new sense of deliverance
Lies in the offing.

November

Gazing at Water Will Not

Quench Your Thirst

Tell you what,
Without so much
As a how-do-you-do
If I see that bloke
With devil well may care smile
Upon his face,
If I catch sight of him
Strolling about the market-place,
A clip on the ear
Is what I might bestow
Upon his personhood.
Is that how I would greet him?
Really?
Perhaps, he won't have a clue
As to what I'm driving at.
No fair, he'll say.
What happened,
That which you did
To my friend,
If what she says is true,
That might be considered
Somewhat inexcusable
And out of line.
She tells me
I cannot forget, can you,
How he left those car keys
On the train?

In a month of Sundays,
How could he do that?
If your heart
Is full of pain
And suffering.
If you
One of many
Who feel
Imprisoned
Within an unfeeling heart
Can you top that?
What is the point
To a life
Half-lived.
From the start,
Well it would be for him
Had you told him
Confiding in him
Everything
Of how you felt.
Or else!
Or else, what?
What else is there?
If your truck
Is that what
Needed hauling
Up the mountain
Telling him what you wanted,
Why not
Call on him.
It might actually calm him.
God-drenched, the truth
Of why you're calling.

Behind his most
Admirable quality,
What gives?
You have every right
To love him
If you chose.
If caring
For another person
Beyond the call of duty's most idolatrous
Blood then, cut to the chase and let him go.

•

Perhaps I drank too many
Cups of wine on Tuesday.
Perhaps I fed too many
Stray cats with milk.
Knowing what I know
Good morning,
How can my body's
Soul-garment
Sustain itself?
To fend for itself,
Catching the lamentation of its sullen sparks?
Must my threadbare soul appear
Horse-whipped for eternity?
In a constant state of caterwauling?
Mourning what's lost?

A pomegranate breaks open
In the offing, a melon ripens.
Peach trees, plum trees, apricot
Trees, all are full of fruit.
Why is the vineyard empty?
Fruit is never counterfeit.
Who wants to reborn in me?
Asks the quail. Does the quail or the dove
Want to return to a world, vast and inviolable,
A world whose leaders have been caught *flagrante delicto?*
Defrauded, denuded, deprived of leaves,
Trees don't dare to talk to one another.
I don't want the world to be used up of all its goodness.
If the world of chattering birds continues
Does every bird on lockdown needs be detained or caged?

NOVEMBER 4

The man looks upon her as his sometime woman,
Slovenly and lowly. Though she is his student, full well
He knows she could turn the Vedas upside down.
While he looks forward to the details of her story,
A boastful man is still half-distracted with fear.
She's the one in need of a teacher.
Besides, in time, the woman might come to provide
Generous sums for the poor and needy. Is that true?
A man and a woman attend church each Sunday.
They defend each other's presence only by playful loyalty.
Stand tall, the man says to the woman.
Stand tall. Is that all? The woman asks the man.
She has been asking the man the same thing
Since last Tuesday morning. Is that all? Says the woman.
If she hesitates before asking him, Chief Plenty-Coups,
Would you consider towing my car up the mountain?
According to the spirits up in the painted sky, you know why
She thinks she is the one who has committed grand larceny.

I will tell you what he misses her
That is what it is so true, that's the why
He reverses the car
And says he's going to hit a snake
Or go backwards into a creek.
All the time, here's what it is,
He misses her, he just misses her.
Her voice is what healed him
Of his darker days and it is her
Presence caused him not to fall
Asleep at the wheel, nor to indulge
In the swing vote. In fact, it was her vote
Causing him to want to sleep with her.
That was it. I'll tell you a thing or two right now.
When she passed out near dead on the floor,
He found out exactly like to be the one
Missing out on her giving her the kiss of life.
I'll tell you what's next to the almighty truth
Of a great god. That's what it is: he misses her.
He just misses her. He was almost in love with her.

NOVEMBER 6

Life is fragile enough without this pick-up-sticks
Element rearing its ugly head; an indelible ink palmprint
Showing up in a painting of a horse flank against a backdrop
Featuring the bluest evening filled with pock-marked stars.
Tiring of thinking it must be a slipped disc,
She skips a chiropractic
Appointment. Her psychic says it's just her nerves.
Her acupuncturist tells her she's too was once afraid of needles.
A pundit tells her it's a subdural hematoma, scar tissue
Imagery accrued from past life karma. Her hairdresser, the one
Explaining to her it's the glue used to mend her violin whereas
The glue she uses to mend her accordion and the lampshade
Inside the bedroom cannot the original culprit, *n'est-ce pas?*
Divorce is the thing most likely to have gotten her slain
In the spirit.
Only god and the prophets know the absolute source:
As the progenitor of a most unlikely and unfortunate scenario:
Did the person calling herself her mother ever get it right?

November 7

It is your birthday and this very day was my due date.
The nurse insulted me; she announced my stretchmarks
Meant the baby came too late to earn myself a nice hot cup of tea.
Of course, there'd been a hospital strike the day before.
Duly reported in the notes, the doctor and his midwife amputees
Were out playing golf in their quarters only one mile distant.
At two am in the morning, what do you expect? Maid service?
Any one of our nursing staff on call could very well
Be engaged with the virulent needs of other customers.
Do you expect them to drop everything on your account?
To come running towards you like a couple of stranded
Tibetan mountain goats?
Predictable as rain, the fact of the matter,
Your husband is not the only person on the planet.
As a first-time parent,
Everyone's husband is known to have a smoke;
It's what helps push the babies out into this blessed world of ours.
The doctor on call, your cousin, wasn't he the one you remember
Telling you to keep in touch?
Why do you like metaphors so much?

NOVEMBER 8

I'm a vegetarian. I know I helped myself to lots of samples
In the shop. It was a job and half. I had my other job
As a psychic on the weekends. I sold my paintings.
When my boyfriend got put in the slammer, I didn't know
What to do. I know didn't make enough on tips.
I sold my painting here and there at fairs, but even
That was not enough to support three children.
It was like the siege of Troy had never ended.

Heart-scalded I am
I've never seen
The little tyke.
I don't even know
Whether she has a cat
Or knows how to ride
A bicycle.
Once a driver told me
He saw her.
Her mother tried
To send me a picture
Of herself as a baby
Passing her herself
Off as the very same grandchild.
With a little scolding,
People often come back.
This daughter of mine
Is an exception.
Some wear a mask.
Some let the mask
Drop from an ear
Used as a coat rack.
Some listen to science.
Some listen to fear.
Although time's winged
Chariot is closing in on us.
At the back of neck

A tingling sensation
Tests the intellect
As a trusted friend.
While vineyard leaves
Thicken and blacken
To ash, we play a game of cribbage.
We play a diddling game of silver spoons
We view how high the stakes
And if the universe will sigh.

When deeds of war
Have the upper hand,
Who has the final say?
A drop of water
From an ewer
Empties a river's flowing
Every jam jar
Filled with plums
Later reverses itself
Until a plum tree drowns
In milk spilling sacerdotal fire.
Ignited with sullen sparks,
Sobbing with longing,
Can I remain comforted
In a sleep that's upside down
Why argue with pestilence,
Fire and flood.
Eyes closed, heavy-lidded and asleep,
Does angelic goodness
Remain unmoved?
Subtracted from the sky,
When songbirds refuse to sing,
When an arrow slips its noose
Reverberating fate,
Thought arrows always miss the mark.
Quit talking about sleights-of-hand
An ant that's drowning in a granary

Is it worth one grain's surrounding
Precinct and lack of trespass
Unmasking its authority's clown?

We have gotten ready for an autumn audition
Dozens of times,
We've courted countless leaves falling down,
The frowning of wings
Kissing uneven ground.
It's been long enough.
When I come to think of it, a very long haul.
Nothing in the greening
Universe could have prepared us
For growing older than a worn rug
Whose tassels
Descend into reckless knotted strings.
Eyebrows, wrinkles, moles and warts,
Beauty's tarnished beauty
Revoked and reworked by dust.
Everything falling into the ground like turnips.
This wine cellar is a very strange one.
When we arrive, are we surprised,
All the wine has been sopped up
By marauding hordes of ants?
Try to pinpoint the source of the perfume
Sensing what's been lost, you cannot.
If Insanity's madness
Unloose a stream of words,
For which there's no retort.
If the sun wears a face of burnished gold,
What of the shadows cowering before a
Honeyed hive or a scorpion pit?
What of the distance in-between has sunk a thousand ships?

In some families
Leaves are not allowed to run riot
They're not even permitted to rot into the ground.
What took you so long?
One family member asks.
Another relative queries
If I turn the other cheek
Whenever a person dies,
Nothing inspires as much as defeat
By default
Inasmuch as,
Whether fully rehearsed or not
No story in a life
Unlived or unaccounted for
Takes as long as an unanswered riddle
Or ivy leaping up to defend a garden
Taking up
Clog dancing
Helps develops strong calves
Reading the Bible
Another hit.
Being lost in infinity's grip,
An additional lobby
Might include
Handwriting analysis,
So, bite your lip.
Reviling your multiple interests,
Go along with ghost-writing
That will take your soul away
Emulate

Whoever stated
What they thought
Was the truth?
We'll go no more a roving
Into the dark night alone?
Is that true?
A man once said
Is it cold where you live?
No one will ever come
And stay with you.
Is that true?
Later, shrugging his shoulders,
Striking is grey beard
He reversed himself.
Wait a minute,
Is that also not true?
I do see someone
Coming to stay with you.
Coming to stay with you
For quite a long time.
Is that true?
Is that also true?

She said
First thing I will do
Is to separate you two.
Alphabet Woman
And Bison woman.
As for Bison Woman
She will sleep
Sleep in the sun room
The screened in porch room
With all the plants.
And Alphabet Woman
You will sleep
In another room
With all the writing machines.
I said
How come?
She said
The older Bison woman,
Can sleep in the sun porch
The screened in room
Among acacia leaves.
But the younger woman,
Alphabet Woman
She stays in the office
She sleeps with the family dog.
Alphabet Woman
Assumed: this must be
A very old fable
Playing out the truth
From the north.
Is this about Ground Hog Day?

NOVEMBER 15

It won't be long before
All the little farms are gone.
All foodstuffs plowed under
Now brick has taken over reform
Pastures filled with cattle grazing
Sheep gathered in clusters,
All these genteel portraits
Have been washed out to sea.

NOVEMBER 16

On the other side of town, it always rains.
On this side, drought, no snow, no rain.
Hath the rain a father or a feathered downpour?
In warmer weather, we used to live under threat of hurricane
When we scrutinize pine trees dancing in the wind,
Nothing actually happens, not here. In the future,
God will look back upon this flawed weather
As some kind of diminutive oversight,
Some kind of innocence has almost taken over
By the immediate ghost of nettle, briar, and thorn.
Something of a deep concern, rages within the body,
Something, the body quite ill-prepared for. As ravens caw,
Don't hesitate to tell us, we don't know why we're here.

Chairs rearrange themselves
As if they are beholden
To no one but invisible parishioners
Attending a church service whose priest
Has long since been abandoned.
Wine waits for those at the table
To consummate their love.
If a marble clock waits for the mantle
To do away with numbers
What kind of birdsong is required?
To singe a cloudless sky?
To run a ship aground?
Melancholy, endlessly seeded
By northern lights, some nights are like this
They shine with merciless stories of fire.
Shifting their hours so that the story of our lives
Will match perfectly with everything that's been said,
Night walks the streets in a black velvet gown.
The bride awaits her departure first, then his.
In the middle of the next night, dogs burst into the room.
See how the midnight stars whirl about in giddy waltzes?
Is there any sign of resistance
From those already attuned to death's indifference?
Now is the time for the sky to swallow up
Every last petal of a flower.
The flower says: he loves me, he loves me not,
The flowers offers this caveat: well,
Not as much as he says he did.
Snuffed out, a candle resets the smoke
Of an earlier incarnation. The candle says"
I am biding my time in frozen oceans of tallow pools.

Coins gathered from a congregation
Ends up being sequestered in a velveteen pouch.
Divested of our walking shoes waiting in the closet,
All of us are in the process
Of inventing reasons to stay perfectly awake and alive
To what is going on. In great profusion, willows nod.
Open-mouthed and comatose,
Someone is sleeping in the parlor.
There is no casket that will hold her body, not now.
The hour when she rises from pressed linens
And great silken quilts, begin falling from her body,
She will count on every hoot owl to own her sense of privilege.

November 18

The debutante must receive her due.
But then again, she's never danced alone.
If she has no guardian angel, it's the same
To her if she does or does not go to war.

We need a plush loveseat
Not a hospital divan. We need a feathered down pillow
Not polyester granules floating in a plastic quilt.
We need a bed that is as wide as a cerulean sky
To lie upon and await the Mysteries from Mycenae.
Yet, if you're not ill and you haven't lost
Your mind, you're simply not worth a penny.
Every week I send a penny to the children's blind home.
Braver people have gone through circumstances of depravity.
They're still going through it. If we're immune
To the wiles of corporate leadership,
Whose members used to sell
Little plots of acreage way up in the mountains of Alaska
On the back of cereal boxes, you might even receive an ounce
Some sacred land deal gone awry
Represented in a shoddy picture of a moose
Drinking from a holy well or a non-polluted drinking fountain,
Promiser the reader immediate ownership.
Upward mobility for clowns.
The Master knows most of the masses are weeping
By themselves because they don't even own
Their mortgage payments. Many drowned bones of horses
Are found at the bottom of a lake. At the time of one's death,
Every story must be foreshortened. Flags are lowered.
Fallen down to half-mast;
That's when god seems half-drunk again.
You cannot even hope to get even with Jupiter this winter,

When lightning, blood-red,
Rains down from heaven's Arctic oven.

The ankles thicken with pock-marked skin
The thinnest lips in the world
Pucker and are lost to wrinkled sighs.
How many eyes do wrinkles clearly carry?
In the old days, no one worried about charity.
About those shadows on the portico,
They never presaged a death
Of a bird's stillborn messenger.
Now death is all about a book of signs.
Lovely palm trees have shriveled to glass.
Though I have played sweet tunes on the cithara
All day for you, those songs never did you any good.
Old age has dusted your hair with snow.
I look across the mottled waters leading
To Stygian shores. Have you ever dared
Sharing with me Hecate's nectar-filled cups?
Can I be the cause of what's missing?
I have woven a visionary quilt for you,
Is that not enough? Though a thief can scale
A high wall, you marvel at his persistence.
I hope the meat keeps me until I get home.

Many will say they behave as
As if they've caught sight of ghosts
But, sadly that's not true.
They act as if fables
Are priceless jewels.
Some folks
Cannot recall the details of a story.
They're too busy lying
About those who do.
Why bother scrutinizing herons
Meditating on a lake?
What's the point of living?
If every piece of furniture is exchanged
For something better, the new divan cushions
Still have gaping holes them.
Though played sweetly,
And strummed again and again,
Both zither and the lyre are hollow
As a dynasty of rotten tree trunks.
A sleepover, a layover in a park,
Is that all I can ask for? I want to die.
Is there any point to living?
My cat remains caught
Beneath the wheels of a rustic car.

In my youth, I used to hasten up
Upon a mountain, for what?
I was used to catching butterflies.
I did not know they were poems.
Fisherman catch fish. Is that bad karma?
Why lease the dawn of a new life
Before an old woman? Though her coffers
Have been crammed with novice offers
Torn from the pages of medieval
Romance novels and the like,
Is there a better kind of a gift?
My crystal pendulum swings yes/no
No/yes. I guess I'll have to wager
Another bet as to what makes deeds
Of kindness sing and sizzle down
The strongest strings of kindness.
Or else, I'll have to let my pendulum
Be buried in the ground.
I have a wishbone. Breaking down
A wishbone's frail ligaments
Will tell me how to stop the heart
That says: I cannot do another thing.
Every promise I have made,
I shall put into practice by a spell.
Don't ask me why I'd enjoy throwing
An apple peel, wide of the mark,
Over my right shoulder. Good luck to alphabets!

I'm only playing with the sum total of my spirit guides.
Guardian spirits, would they ever bother
Bullying a flying ant, a gnat, or a flea?
Even when the wind changes direction,
Never uncouth or discourteous, such guardians
Seeded by deeds of affectionate compassion.
Deepening dreams of Divinity's blameless source,
What of a soul's alignment to professed vows?
Bearing witness to my supplicant's wounded cries
Without Wisdom begetting gratitude within,
Without a curse on bravado's ego, how can I get by?
O Divine Intelligence, do you believe
I've taken leave of all of my senses?
Why linger by a winking hearth?
Have I lost sight of the torchlight?
Trained on all the soul's accouterments
Ensconced in the upper room?

When the timeless rime refuses to chime
With birds singing in cornfields,
Take time to stop and scrutinize complaints.
It is said the birds were not thirsty enough.
Their singing had become commonplace
Knowledge. Nothing melodic was sung aloud.
Is that the result of panning for too much gold?
Should ignorant men be found weeping
Into their soup tureens or beards
When things don't turn out
Exactly as they'd planned.
Why flout the law of averages?
Even on a moonlit wall,
At midnight, the moon cannot disguise
Her love of coins banging on her heels
Disguising her love of justice. For ravens,
That's something worth crowing about
Even it makes a mincemeat out of poetry.
Rejoicing means looking out for beauty,
For something otherworldly and mysterious.
Why rebuke those already accursed?

November 24

Hope the meat keeps until I get home.
You think I calibrate sweet distances
Between two cypress trees. They fail define
The sense of pilgrimage I must make.
Every waiter knew of my aunt from Timbuctoo.
She always took her afternoon tea and scones
At the Café de Romero. Pre-existing among
All the peoples of the book, she may have softened
As regards her view of love. A poet, she had been
Divorced for centuries. Clacking gold-rimmed castanets
Singing into the little lips of burning leaves, she whispers
Transparent are the wings of the multicolored birds
Dancing in the desert. When camels tilt their heads
You can almost come to believe they know the truth.
Camels ruminate on prayers of a forgiving god.
Living outside in a field next to the plenitude
Of the Café de Romero has never been easy for anyone.
She had perfected the sense of fending for herself forever.
In all likelihood, she lived the life of a story of a sparrow.
Why had the meat and marrow of her dreaming shadow
Been foreshortened?

NOVEMBER 25

Goblets of wine were overturned
On a boudoir table belonging to Henry's Dad,
Beside the chipped coffee mugs,
Beside stone amulets from the Hopi and the Hidatsa,
Henry often sang to his player-piano.
Deconstructing all his attempts at consciousness,
Every woman that came within six feet of him,
He loved as if death never dwelt within the confines
Of the adobe village
He was reported to have come from.
A sense of belonging
Eluded him like a sparrow
Already flown from the branch
Was it yesterday or will it be tomorrow?

I told myself I didn't know
My boss was on the phone.
I didn't know he'd stoop so low.
Not when I was with child
I had rocked another child
To sleep all night in the old
Rocker on the porch. I don't know
 Whether he sought to belittle me
Out of pity or a deferred sense
Of gratitude. Maybe it was not a question
Of whether he used land o' lakes butter
On his bread for the evening meal or not,
But didn't he delight in calling me
On the company phone to test
My knowledge of spelling.
This was before the engine of the internet
And so forth. I can't recall whether
I admitted I knew it was his voice.
Once I told him I knew it was him
And was not a customer. But he ignored
That part of the conversation, well yes,
Up to a point, that is. One occasion
I asked him: what do you want correctly
Spelled this time? Alphabet soup?
Of course, for that remark
I did not have any intention
Of getting fired.

Though I had to spell the word
Sesquipedalian first. So, this then
Is that poem of which I am most proud
It is all about me getting fired and my having
Been a single parent with two children
And no paycheck and no sign of a wedding dress.
I suppose all of us may live for whatever
Future may lie ahead for in the spring
The sight of a flowering tree is a most welcome
Sight even for those of us possessing scarcely any eyesight.

NOVEMBER 27

I can hear the horse hoofs clacking
On cobblestones. I am not sure whether
This is a dream of something that is coming.
You know most of my coins are counterfeit
And the one stamp in my stamp collection
Hadn't been cancelled so it is worthless.
But this is not a poem about being or non-being.
The candles on the birthday cake are self-igniting.
The frosting is a knockout coconut
On this day, life seems simply briefly gorgeous
And I was not in need of an umbrella or a parasol.

NOVEMBER 28

I was in the middle of making a meal
For one hundred people.
I went into labor right during
The kneading-of-the-dough ceremony.
After that, I only had to worry
What does it take to feed one person?

Picked-a-fine-time-to-leave-me, Lucille
Might have been a horse and not a woman.

November 30

Money gone
Casino savings blown
On one machine
A hurricane brings home
Plenty of pigeons
Surrendering an empty plate.
When noble members
Of the rabble disappear
Who will shout present
Present during a roll call
I'm glad to be here
In a premonition
About a roll call occurring
Prior to auctioning off
The empty plate
Or a heap of
Decisive remarks
Which follow
Most ordinary lessons
In elocution.
Those ordinary
Conversations,
Of late

December

Breaking the Mustard Seed

Into Twenty Pieces of Gold

DECEMBER 1

It's not about being chased
Our of your own back yard
It's not about pointing the finger
At the one who is believed to be the guilty party
It's about a trickster named *Nanabozho*
Who wanted to be born on both sides
Of the tracks. Having one foot in two
Camps, does that make it any easier
To be slain in the spirit?
Everyone in the universe should have
Been apprised through a Raven's dreamtime.
A lighting strike, a tornado, a cyclone,
A fire, a whale detained on a beach.
An arctic fox cannot proclaim the answer.
A four-way stop sign doesn't make matters
Any easier to decode.

DECEMBER 2

Canaries don't fit in back pockets, not usually anyway.
Unlike those sovereign coins you win at a Casino, though
Sadly, though they may sense
You are an imposter or a ventriloquist,
You can safely carry those birds from room to room
In your right hand.

Love birds have no patience. Stammering,
Can they avoid hearing statisticians' quarrels
Over the evening news?
Unlikely to spend the rest of their days in limbo,
Whether still in the process of rinsing breakfast dishes,
Is of no real concern. Chattering,
Love birds draw up a number of absurd rules.

Like Nanabozho, canaries are of a totally different species.
Speaking in a foreign tongue unknown to mankind's relatives,
Intelligible only to llamas conversant with mid-level chakras,
Perching on a bird-swings at higher elevations, canaries rock.

Failing to perform those little Mexican hat dances of theirs
Out of acts of pure desperation
Or even as primordial acts of devotion
After surviving countless fires Santa Rosa, California,
Canaries will deign to wait until the Long-Playing-Record
Is placed on a turntable in the front parlor. In acts of gratitude,
Canaries will sing a one-of-a-kind Rumanian Gypsy songs

Such as would knock your socks and your head buds off.
Certain parts of your body, you can now eliminate,
Once and for all.

Canaries ask that we love them again as we once did before
For no particular reason other than when it is raining, it rains
With the softest of reckless feathers, each one carrying a note.
We are waiting for hopeful music
From the dominion of our demons.

December 3

In first learning how to speak about what
We think we sense is part of our anatomy,
We must also learn all the melodies by heart
Learn how one tribe and then another
Was begotten by word particles
Molecules that, on occasion,
Incited us all to riot because we longed to keep company
And never break ranks with a strange cacophony of leaves.
Refusing so to speak to one another's
Presence in this precarious and fragile world,
If the book required something different of us
Would someone please let us know.
We were not fully aware of ourselves
To know what that really was.
I want to be brave enough to open
The book of the heart and reason
With the enemy. Nothing is the same.
Conversations, long overdue, are toppled
By deliberate masks of indecision and divisiveness.
Just for show does the bogeyman wear a mask
With green turtles racing towards the ocean
Painted over the entire width and breadth of the fabric?
Whatever we lack, let us know exactly what that is.
Can the pages of a book entice us to be much stronger
Because it has snow leopards running all over
The fevered fabric of their pages that will not end our lives?

December 4

What you have in mind are images
I've never thought of envisioning.
I want to escape your eyes. A little
In your eyes wants me to resume living,
For how long? Why do you continue
Hastening a portfolio of dreaming images?
I see you seeing me when asleep
And dipping with your wings into tall grasses
Lifting from a cornfield's keep. No one ever need record
These prayers.

December 5

How long can a child live?
A child lives long enough, enough years
To hoodwink the voice of an opera star. Why fear envy?
Why revoke suffering long enough to slice a singer's throat.
I told my daughter, don't sing, your voice could become
Attached to a furious brush fire. Why not learn to cherish love?
You can always learn to play the violin? A cicada persists.
Her voice breaks off into a whisper, what if my arm?
What if my back? What if a common song sparrow
Refuses to sing the grace notes diminuendo?
What if my brain merges with angel fish lit only by a coral reef?
What if I can't get back to the place of belonging, where
I began, and then left off? A long time ago, leave-taking
Broke my back, I said. I never danced again.
I never returned to the place where I left off,
Isn't that same place, my grandmother,
Left off her tapestry sewing? Isn't that place, the same,
As the mountain my grandfather left off
His donkeys and his goats,
My parents never let me back into the rooms of their house.
They always said they would. In any case, they did not.
Love is as illogical as my sleeping thighs.

December 6

The gray ghost of the mind
What does it do?
As an after-thought,
In filagree of smoke,
Hidden among petals of a flower,
Words shatter all too easily
Words happen to hold back sorrow
And the great wind that folds our bodies
Back into positions only dancers know
And a scarecrow perched on snow-topped ledges.
In adjacent rooms of several dreams
Where there exist plenty of contingency plans for operations:
Sheltering a duck blind, in a tent, in a lean to, in a shed, in a hut.
Seeing the wolf take the deer into his mouth
Ending the deer's life. For the life of me, I can't forget.
That was enough. As for me, I didn't want to go
On the hunt, at least, not in the company of others.

December 7

You'd know you had a good class
When you'd pass out
Like a dead person
On the floor.
I didn't do a workout
Worth anything
Unless
That happened.
I couldn't have done
Better or more
Once I told my mother
I was a sweet doggie.
After all, we had an Irish setter
That was used to hauling me
Around in a sleigh
At the height of winter
Whenever we went toboggining.
More than once,
When the sleigh with me in it
Became used to tipping over
Again, I would pass out.
The same way
As in my ballet class.
My mother found it comical.
I often wondered
What happened to all
The snow

Clinging to the outside of the window.
Later on,
When I was older,
Than two years old,
H. told me
About his mother
In her Laplander's hat
Disappearing
Into the ocean
In Iceland
When he was a child
Of about two years.
I wondered
Whether
It was the same
As losing consciousness
Or about not seeing
What you cared about most
Ever swimming back
Into view.
H. also said
Whenever it snowed
He thought everyone
In a town
Would back out
Of agreeing
To being

And non-being
Having little or no choice
About turning back
Sometimes life
Is about coming to.
The body is totally beyond the schooling,
The stammering of the six senses.
Soldiering on
The body holding my heart
Knows a steep hill
Even without toboggining.
I used to always wish
For April
And the blooming
Of the wild peach tree
Creating new snow-blossoming
All over again.

Because I looked older
Than you imagined
And was not
In a wheelchair
About years passing
And old age
All you said was
Mom, are you
All right?
You look
Like dad.
But you knew
Dad was not my father
Nor my mother my mother
Yet, as your mother,
I always said
Yes, I'm all right
But I was not
You knew
I was lying
My ears are old.
You know I keep
Holding them
Away from the sides
Of my head
As if knowing about them
They always were something

Belonging
To someone else
And had gone out of fashion
Like old veiled old hats and death

December 9

Tethered to the ghost
Of this world
We want to walk away
A platform of lies
Has been built up
Over the course
Of several years
A little string
Holds the bodies
Of dead people on earth
Another string
Holds the body
Of living people
On earth
When writing
This poem
I watched this morning
As a spider spat out a string
Of spittle
Full throttle
Shot down to the floor
And moved again
Among the people
Faster than the wind
It would be wrong
To foster any imagining
About the way in which

I would put him out
In the desert
Where woodpeckers
Would delight
In finding him
Spinning posterity's yarn
Inside a tree trunk.

He kept talking
About Allen Ginsberg
To the elder senior taxi driver
Who knew Allen G. very well
Probably in fact he knew him
Just as well
As the professor did
Anyway, the two men
Kept the conversation
Moving for such a long time
In memory's upper rooms
The driver began slowing his song
And the meter kept talking
About breaking down its numerical voice
Into multi modal syllabic content
Where discretionary viewer monitoring became advisable
For both men it was all about the time they first met
And the last time they met
In San Francisco.

December 11

The cards were stacked
Against me
Inasmuch as I never asked
Why the monk
Asked me to dance at all
I couldn't tell
What he was really asking
I only told him
If temptation held him
Briefly for a moment's trek
By the scruff of the neck
From the beginning of time
The mother cat was dropping off
The kitten right here
Outside the hotel front door
In that way, if chimes ever knew how to rime
Before they were ever asked so to do
They would stop
Stopping for definite certain on a dime.

DECEMBER 12

Don't emphasize
The wounded bird needs healing.
It is absurd to pretend healing will take place
When healing is a cataclysmic enterprise for some
Don't estimate degrees of snowfall in a season of autumn
When every leaf is not the same
A heart's rallying cry for freedom
Is not measured by the number of drumbeats
Is not the same as when a trumpeter swan's decoy
Is spotted on a lake or a pond or slow-moving river
If the swan dodges cloudbursts and supernovas
Exploding over a swampland
Like spindrift flying in windstorm
Feathers cut from geese would better swim into a quilt
Those that were needed for an eiderdown

Receive a Botox blessing
From the keeper of the keys
Receive a tummy tuck
A nouveau hip
A nouveau knee
Yet nothing works.
The same soul
Bumps up against the ribcage
And wonders how it got inside that cage
Detained for another year.

I don't want the turtle
To carry on its back
The weight of all sorrows
I don't want the turtle
To carry an entire adobe village
On its back. To come tracking
Out of winter leaning against
Furred collars in snow
Leaning against ledges
Leaning on ladders
Lifting up to god knows where.
I don't want the turtle
To carry on its back
Those distant dreams
We could never seem to fulfill.

I got prepared to meet the master
At camp where I danced the part
Of Coppelia over and over
I also had a part in Babes in Toyland
My road would end
At the bottom of the heap
I got prepared
When I finally saw
The master I ran
For my life.

Nobody dies.
Nobody gets born
Can you save yourself
From growing old?
Once the harpist
Became hunched over
Nobody listened.
Nobody dies.
Nobody is born.
Close your eyes.
Without growing wise
Bring me back
To the beloved
Who has never been born.
Close your eyes.

No other world
Is worth referencing.
Souls have their own world.
The sputtering blue light
Of gas lamps,
The only thing that matters.
Are people afraid of their own cooking?
Is that what the soul fears most?
In a garden of thimbles,
In a garden of knives,
The luxury of paper flowers
Is quite noticeable.

December 18

The self-defeating places
Of the heart:
He loves me
He loves me not.
While stars whirl
And evaporate
In the morning,
A wonderful light
Will emanate
No matter
Whether
The poem
Is ever finished.
I long to witness
Sea-horses
With no latch-key
Children.

December 19

I will never die
I will never get old.
A spider skates
From my writing table.
I never saw one
Like this before.
Like an old man
He skids, he slips on a skating rink.
He sits, he waits and then he leaps
Into any one of several escape routes.
Decides the string of the world
Is his vine
As he chimes to the rime
Of his spittle
And it is too late
He's dodging
All the fallout from the decisions
He must make.
That's when the spider
Drifts to the end of the rope.
The world is in an uproar
Over that. The miniature
Sea-horses all end up
In the same world
Of the novel
Never quite completed.

DECEMBER 20

The declension of moths
On the kitchen screen
Is enough.
It's getting colder.
I will start knitting
Again.
Birthday presents
Like this are a must.
Knickers will be worn
From the Boulder Thrift Store.
Isabella wrote me a letter
Telling me her sciatic nerve
Isn't getting any better.
She is afraid of needles
So, she puts off going
To an acupuncturist.
It's a trick the brain plays on you
I write back. You are not
Getting any younger.
Later on, your brain forgets to play
The trick of going into another pain channel
When the monsters come back,
It is too late.
Your back goes out again.
When you cannot tie your shoes
You risk the fact
Leg warmers may become passé.

DECEMBER 21

If I see people
That are not there
I have a health problem.
This is not supernatural
Gravel is not thrown
At a window during
A séance to create trouble
It offers legitimacy for story-tellers
Nothing is indicative of a psychosomatic
Or a structural inhibition
So much for my friend
Who decided to throw
Herself in front of a moving car
For all she cared,
It could have been a train
On one of her whistle-stop operatic tours.
If I prefer a rocking chair
To a straight-backed chair,
There are census inspectors
Who believe you're at risk
Of a slipped disc
Not the intense rivalry of families
Nor the metempsychosis of metaphors.
You can keep the dogs at bay
Only for so long
Too many back stories
Persist in handbooks

The midwifery of narcissism
Ends up
As a stage play
Or a charade
Your money
Or your life.

December 22

Why did the angel
Tell me come back
Go back! Don't stay
In the tunnel!
Your golden string
Will fray.
Your mind
May slip into a muddle.
I pleaded with the angel I have two children
They are in this country. I don't want to
Be caught malingering ad infinitum.
She said: don't look back.
Don't blame anyone
For your condition.
Remember this,
When you return to earth
You will sit by a different hearth.
It will not be the same.
I asked the angel
Whence she came.
Did she know everything?
Why did the elderly Sikh
Stop me in the middle
Of the street. Why did he tell me
I had unusual karma. I thought karma
Was like an exotic humming bird brooch
Or a bracelet fitting around my wrists and ankles

Like a good luck charm or an amulet.
I knew karma was something
To be reckoned with. If you failed
To follow the dictates of your conscience,
Fate would beget more fate and time
Rake over your life. A tree or a rock
Could end up falling on you
Or your beloved. I didn't want
To ignore or stretch out the possibilities
That availed me of so many breaths,
So many street lights, so many debts.
Is that why the Sikh told me I must
Be willing to produce two children?
Now that I cannot answer, my sweet.
The angel said. Now tomorrow
Be sure to go back to the restaurant
Where you work. You don't want
Then thinking you're incapacitated.
Continue your job of flipping chappatis
In the back room. It's comparatively quiet.
No one will disturb you there.
I'll put you are on the prayer list.
Nothing in your life will go amiss.
That said, the angel left.

December 23

Behind lace framing the window sheds it's light.
In some way, hope is spread about the place.
I told Aunt Myrna I was not sure
When I could take time to visit her.
I had so many duties keeping me
At home. She didn't like to hear
That news. You're the only one
I see, she told me, and, without you,
I see no one. Left to my own devices,
I could go to the dogs, my spirit
Could dry up, and wither. Quite
Easily, I could go bonkers.
A flower in an unkempt garden
Is the one that wants nourishing.
Careless, reckless, and carless, I live.
When it comes right down to it,
To my knowledge, no dictionary exists
As old as the wind in the pine trees.

DECEMBER 24

Until we had a chimney fire in Duluth,
We used to put out shoes or stockings
Around the hearth. Well-worn
And well used, the shoes were as big
As rowboats abandoned on a shore.
Mother used to stuff the stockings
With ribboned offerings of fruit,
And chocolate. Today, the custom
Isn't followed. We go to church.
We're tired of hearing the same sermon,
Nothing is the same. Generations of women
Must have known what was about to happen.
Among gingham aprons, is there some mistake?
In their more than perfect calculations,
The body count must stand for something,
It used to mean there was a war on in some
Far-off exotic place.
The ledger book holds
The sounds of loons on the lake.
A porcelain body breaks.
In the afternoon, we used to fall asleep on the sofa.
What keeps us lonely for ourselves?
A full moon?
A full array of plush cushions?
We're wide awake.
Aquamarine, the color of the sky. Geese mark
The occasion of Christmas with a single cry.

The snow has lain on the ground
For over a fortnight.
In Chicago,
Stars shine brighter than before
Indigo and russet red
The color of bright flowers
On the side of the road.
What can be said
Has already been said.
We take delight
In the meaning
Of shadows.
That's only
Because in the morning,
We have seen the light.
It is that simple?
Tomorrow is a warning
As to what is to come.
Let the perfume of your hands
Be proof.
A god may still
Exist in the sky.

December 26

Before mankind
Was undone by engaging in big wars
Marauders,
Outlaws,
And warrior-kings
Were content
To keep on circling
The smallest wagon trains
In the history of the desert.
Thus, frontier settlers
Members
Of the esteemed wagon
Train division of scholars,
Those detained
In the middle
Of the circle,
Began serving
 As the focal point
By default.
Don't you think
Those scholars
Always agreed
To be encircled?
Life seemed
More exciting that way.
When we were youngsters,
Aunt Jessie cautioned us:

Live and let live.
People, she said,
Have many choices.
Different people
Do different things
Is what she told us.
Some people just love
To play cops and robbers.
In makeover moves
During the course
Of their fevered lives,
Those folks never
Learned to leave
Well enough alone.
When left to their own
Devices, with too much
Time on their hands,
Life is bound
To catch up with them
Until they end up poorly sick.
A long time ago, these people
Should have learnt
To take up knitting
Or some kind of wholesome
Activity, charitable and kind.
Rendering the world
A better place.
Freebooters
Thought they
Were people
Just like that.

December 27

Aunt Jessie never died of the plague.
She did not die of influenza.
She did not catch any of those childhood
Diseases.
Scrutinizing the disc of the sun
Never blinded her. A drowning man
Never asks for anything
He simply drowns.
Beggaring,
The entire ocean
In acceptance
Of his reward.
What's more,
Every droplet
Evaporates
In clouds
Or dissipates in whispered
Threads of forgotten sky ethers.
Since the expiration date
On self-expression
Has expired,
No library
Card was ever needed.
Look back on your
Life and remain inspired
By every single action encountered.
As a baker continuously kneads

Another piece of dough,
Don't be inconsolable.
If you are not inspired
By his activity,
God will not be incited
To indulge in acts of riotous living,
Or to judge them any of them
And how they started.

December 28

There would have been a time
When I would have been amazed.
Now I am not.
Life goes on.
I am not surprised.
I like
To keep the weight
Of the unknown symphony,
As mysterious as possible.

Play the fiddle again.
I don't have cancer.
Play the fiddle again
I am still a folk-dancer.
I don't have cancer.

December 30

Using flawless details, coyotes would have gladly explained
Everything that was happening in this world of ours
In going over and reviewing the particulars of their to-do lists
At this time, they are perfectly capable of complete clarity.
Yet, coyotes cannot quite explain what is happening.
In fact, they have held off announcing it was a UFO
Causing the present problem. They are still yowling under
A full moon. At certain stages, they know someone
Messed up, but they are not prepared to announce
Prayer-meeting night or cross-referenced calendars
In their date-books.
Shell-shocked, they know they are not responsible
For degrees of fallout.
Nor for our moving about like sleepwalkers
In these dark and evil days.
Horses are even asking to take a share in our seeking the truth.

We will dismiss the action of the bear
Trying to catch the leaping salmon in Klamath Falls
We will forgive the missed opportunity
When the claw didn't quite catch the flawed fish
And the scales failed release to his jaw.
That day, the stars refused whirling in the sky.
The Hippocratic oath simply did not come into play.

ABOUT AUTHOR
ELIZABETH MARTINA BISHOP

. . . .

Elizabeth Martina Bishop is currently attending Salve Regina's MFA program under the direction of New York Times award-winning novelist, Ann Hood. Bishop has penned over seventy books and is currently working specifically on a series of oracle books.

Some of these works include: When a Window Opens, When a Door Opens, When a Spirit Opens, and When a Cafe Opens.

Each oracle book contains a collection of individual poems written as a specific expansive message specifically tailored for each day of the year; thus, in that way, readers can look up their birthday poems and find a bit of synchronicity if it still exists in this computerized and highly digitalized and inspiring universe of ours.

In future, Bishop plans to perform readings for the blind and to make audio recordings of her poems.

For a listing of most of her publications, please refer to her website at www.elizabethmartina bishop.com.
You may also find her books listed on amazon.com

Made in the USA
Middletown, DE
11 November 2020